WHEELS & DEALS

WHEELS & DEALS

Bill Richardson

Acknowledgements

In writing this book, I'd like to acknowledge the help of Philippa Cull, who listened to my tapes, corrected them, even when I wasn't wrong, and typed the transcript. Philippa e-mailed them on to Clive Lind, previously editor of *The Southland Times* and *The Evening Post*, Wellington, and presently editor of *The Manawatu Evening Standard*, who knocked them into shape.

Bill Richardson

Frontispiece photograph: From coaches to concrete . . . the Richardson family business began in the coaching business in Wyndham, Southland, in 1878. It now extends to large readymix concrete interests in Auckland.

© 1999 Bill Richardson

This book is copyright. Except for the purposes of fair reviewing, no part of this publication may be reproduced or transmitted in any form without permission in writing from the publisher.

First Impression   1999 – 143645
Second Impression 2000 – 146408
Third Impression   2000 – 148320
Fourth Impression 2001 – 151897
Fifth Impression   2001 – 52836
Sixth Impression   2003 – 70799

ISBN 0-473-06278-X

Published and printed by Craig Printing Co. Ltd,
PO Box 99, Invercargill, New Zealand.
Email: sales@craigprint.co.nz Website: www.craigprint.co.nz

Contents

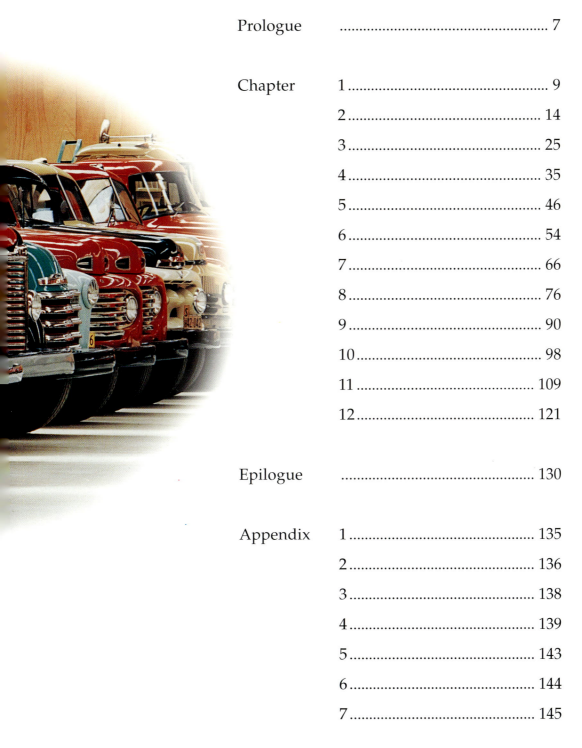

Prologue		7
Chapter	1	9
	2	14
	3	25
	4	35
	5	46
	6	54
	7	66
	8	76
	9	90
	10	98
	11	109
	12	121
Epilogue		130
Appendix	1	135
	2	136
	3	138
	4	139
	5	143
	6	144
	7	145
Index and Sources		146

To Harold

Prologue

I'M BILL RICHARDSON. My business is based in Invercargill, the southernmost city in New Zealand. It's called H W Richardson Group Ltd and it's a holding company, the largest private operator of our type in the country. At last count we had 56 operations in 42 different locations throughout the North and South Islands. We employ about 550 people. I like to think that, even though it bears my name and initials, it's their business as well. The simple truth is that, without them, I wouldn't have a business.

We're based on transport. We have about 350 large trucks bearing the colours of our various interests on the roads day and night. They're hard to miss – from the cream and green trucks of Southern Transport to the bright blue and yellow vehicles of Allied Concrete. From small beginnings we now turn over about $150 million a year. It would be fair to say that trucks – old and new – are my passion as well as my job. I buy trucks, they keep our business going and, more recently, I've decided to collect them as well.

This is my story and it's also the story of my family and the people who have worked with us over the years. Sure, there are two sides to every story but I'd be surprised if many people disagreed with what you're about to read.

Let me start by saying that I was blessed to be born into a family that, first and foremost, cared about being a family. The advantages that flow from that can't be calculated. I was also lucky to be born into a family that loved being in business. So I didn't just learn about right and wrong from my parents. I also learned from a very early age, in good times and bad, about what the business meant to the welfare of our family and all those who worked for us.

It's no exaggeration to say we lived the business. Dad didn't leave our Inglewood Road home in the morning and go to work in some remote office or building. Our business was right next door to our house, down the garden path and through the gate. Literally, I was to follow in Dad's footsteps after I'd married and my wife and I moved into the family home. My office is still next door.

From a business viewpoint I chose a different route to my father. However, I knew Dad not just as a parent but also as a businessman. He shared his business with us, and my mother was happy to see and protect us in that close environment.

There were other influences, of course – relatives, other businessmen, the people who worked for Dad and the friends I made. There were also my teachers at school, not that I was a great scholar.

"Non scholae sed vitae discimus – Not for school but for life we learn" – is the motto of Southland Boys' High School, in those days the secondary school in Invercargill for the scholastically and theoretically inclined, rather than the practical. I obviously didn't appreciate the motto's subtlety as one day, outside its imposing brick building, I watched in fascination as trucks and other machinery reconstructed Herbert Street.

"You won't learn a lot doing that," said a teacher who saw me. He was both right and wrong. At the time, yes, he had a point. But as my life developed his comment was hugely ironic. I did learn a lot from watching and working with trucks.

I also had some God-given gifts to help me through life and they went some way towards overcoming my lack of scholastic achievement. I had a mind for details and determining which were important and which were not. From an early age I liked to study the small print and the figures, such as the specifications of the various parts of the machinery that my father bought for the business. And in the varied interests that my father had I could envisage what was possible and what was not. In the details lay the clues to what could be achieved. It also helped that I have a methodical mind and like to store all the details in an orderly fashion.

And I was naturally curious. Without curiosity you are inclined to accept what is, rather than learn what's possible, which is the difference between a follower and a leader. In time I was to learn how to apply the knowledge I gained.

Luckily I was a good listener. My upbringing helped, of course, with Dad and other adults feeling free to speak in my presence. Perhaps subconsciously I respected that and realised we had two ears and one mouth in rough proportion to how often you should use either. People like to talk and usually there is something to learn, either directly or indirectly. Whether they are speaking with wisdom or talking rubbish is in many circumstances irrelevant. It's important to listen first, then consider and, when appropriate, act upon what you hear. You can apply the wisdom and sometimes learn from people who talk more than they listen.

Until they show me otherwise I believe in people and hope in turn that the people I meet and deal with will believe in me. Most people, in my experience, are essentially honest, wanting only to be treated with respect and dignity. Treat them like that and, almost always, they will treat you similarly. And surely one of life's greatest rewards and securities is to live and work with others in mutual respect.

Our branch of the Richardson family tree began in New Zealand in humble circumstances. Six generations later I'd like to think we still know humility but we are grateful for the opportunities that have been offered to us as a family and to the business with which our family is so closely associated. We have been lucky, but we have also been game enough to take chances and therefore made some of our own luck. We have persevered when others might have given up. We have made many friends, but others have disliked us. We have experienced huge successes and found great happiness. And we have suffered through our tragedies.

But let's start at the beginning.

1

MORE THAN 120 YEARS AGO, on 8 February 1878, a 22-year-old man arrived at the Southland town of Wyndham, located at the junction of the Mimihau Stream and the Mataura River, and so began our recent family history. He was my great grandfather, Samuel Richardson, and like all New Zealanders, of whatever colour or creed, he had come from somewhere else. Samuel was from the parish of Drummall, County Antrim, Ireland, and he settled in New Zealand without looking back much at all.

County Antrim consists of some 3046 square kilometres in the north-eastern corner of Northern Ireland, just across the North Channel from the Mull of Kintyre in Scotland. Distance, slow means of transport and urgency in re-establishing his life meant links to his homeland were bound to be tenuous. Within a generation or two they ceased to exist. The Richardsons were not great correspondents.

The reasons why Samuel Richardson chose New Zealand over other countries in a century when vast numbers of immigrants flowed from Britain, Europe and Asia to build new worlds somewhere else can only be guessed. The most obvious reason was opportunity. Communications by today's standards might have been crude and slow but word of mouth and newspapers were still remarkably effective. Ireland's greatest export is its people and hundreds if not thousands of young Irish men and women were to do what Samuel did.

Young Samuel had wanted to come to New Zealand some five years earlier. The brother of a friend was emigrating to the British colony in the South Pacific and Samuel begged to be allowed to go as well. His pleas got him nowhere, as could be expected because he was only 17, but the brother kept in touch. He had become a saddler in Wyndham and, at the age of 22, Samuel set sail for that town on the other side of the world.

He arrived 38 years after the signing of the Treaty of Waitangi and at a time when the Southland and New

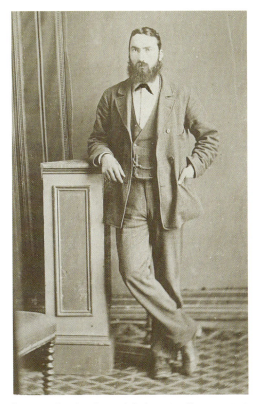

Samuel Richardson settled in Wyndham in 1878 and began our branch of the family.

NEW ZEALAND.

COPY OF REGISTER OF MARRIAGE.   H 9568

1882   Marriage in the District of Lower Mataura

No.	When and where married.	Names and Surnames of the Parties.	Ages.	Rank or Profession	Condition of Parties:— 1. Bachelor or Spinster (or as case may be). If Widower or Widow. 2. Date of Decease of former Wife or Husband.	Birthplace.	Residence. 1. Present. 2. Usual.	Parents. Father's Name and Surname (1), and his Rank or Profession (2).	Mother's Name (1), and Maiden Surname (2).
	Thursday 13th July 1882 Private Residence of Robert Duncan Wyndham	Samuel Richardson	26	Coach Driver	1. Bachelor 2.	Randelstown Antrim Ireland	1. Wyndham 2. Wyndham	1. Robert Richardson 2. Farmer	1. Jane 2. Fenton
		Sarah Anderson Cruickshank	19		1. Spinster 2.	Botriphne Banffshire Scotland	1. Wyndham 2. Wyndham	1. Archibald Cruickshank 2. Farmer	1. Helen 2. Douglas

Married, after the delivery to me of the Certificate required by the Marriage Act, 1880, by James Henry, Officiating Minister [or Registrar].

This Marriage was solemnized between us,   In the presence of us,

Samuel Richardson   Richard Horne, Wyndham, Coach Driver
Sarah Anderson Cruickshank   Agnes Cruickshank

I hereby certify that the above is a true copy of an entry of Marriage in the records of my office. Given under my hand at Wellington, this 14th day of September, 1929.

[The fee for this certificate is half-a-crown.]   Registrar-General.

The marriage certificate of my great grandparents dating back to 1882.

Zealand economy ranged between boom and bust. The great gold booms of the 1860s were well gone, and farming was hindered by a lack of exporting opportunity. Not until 1882 would the first shipment of frozen mutton make its way precariously to London. Had he listened, Samuel would have heard many doom and gloom tales among the stories of boundless opportunity.

But choose New Zealand he did. The reason he chose Wyndham is perhaps more obvious. He knew somebody there. Geographically and climatically there were more attractive places to start life anew. Samuel came from a land settled throughout history by the Scots and the English, an island which had seen its fair share of bloodshed. And he came to a town named in memory of bloodshed. Wyndham had been named after General Windham, hero of the unsuccessful assault on Redan in the Crimean War. For good measure those who handed out names in those days also called a nearby district Redan, after the event, and many of the streets in Wyndham itself reflected that war, including Crimea and Nightingale.

Wyndham was a farm, postal and commerce centre. Situated 6km east of Edendale, 32km south of Gore and 42km east of Invercargill, it served a sprawling district over southern Southland, parts of South Otago and beyond. Its significance was its proximity to the Mataura River and the crossings allowed there, although the river was renowned for its flooding and occasional treachery. Wyndham, with a population of between 300 and 400, boasted stores, hotels and comparative civilisation. By country town standards, the town and the services it provided were substantial in Samuel's day.

Samuel was a country boy, with a family background of farming. For the first three years he worked for Frank King, a ploughing contractor, walking across the district's flat or rolling paddocks behind horses which pulled the plough as the sawmilling industry for which the district was renowned cleared the land to make way for sheep and dairy farms. He must have been reasonably good at ploughing to have remained there so long. But he also had ambition. Unwittingly, perhaps, he began the family tradition of looking for opportunities when he gave up the plough about 1881 to work for one R A Elliott, the proprietor of livery and coaching stables in Wyndham.

Initially Samuel drove a coach to Edendale and managed the stables behind the offices of The Wyndham Farmer, a local newspaper, and he fell in love. One year after he began his new job, at the age of 26, he married 19-year-old Sarah Anderson Cruickshank. Sarah had a similar history to Samuel. She had been born in Botriphne, Banffshire, Scotland, and had accompanied her married sister to the new colony in 1878, arriving in Otago aboard the vessel Wellington. Soon after, sister, husband and Sarah arrived in Wyndham.

By all accounts my great grandmother was a sturdy soul who had no pretensions in life. She lived for her family and her friends. Later it would be written of her: "She had a well-stored mind, being a great reader of informative literature. This gave her a wide outlook on life. Of a placid temperament, she was charitable towards the failings of others, which made her respected by all and beloved by her intimates."

My great grandfather and a fellow workmate, Richard Horne, became good friends. Richard was a witness to his wedding and a year after that event, Samuel, Richard and Edward Challis bought Elliott's business, the laboriously handwritten agreement attesting: "I, the undersigned R A Elliott, agree to sell to Richard Horn (sic), Samuel Richardson and Edward Challis my right and goodwill of the line of coaches trading between Edendale and Wyndham and Wyndham and Fortrose . . ."

In their business venture the three men took possession of 26 horses, one four-horse coach, one bus, one wagonette, one double buggy, one single buggy and one spring trap. They also owned four sets of coach harnesses, one double set of buggy harnesses, one single set of harness, a similar single set, a set of trap harness and four saddles and bridles. To feed and keep the animals the deal also included two stacks of oaten hay situated on Elliott's leasehold section, 400 chaff bags and leases for paddocks and stable. The price was £501-5-0, or $1002.50 in today's dollars and cents, a considerable sum for the times. Elliott agreed he would not start in the coaching business within 30 miles of Wyndham for the next four years.

Samuel went about building his business and raising a family. He became the sole owner when Horne died. What happened to Challis is a mystery. Then, as now, business partnerships dissolved easily.

Large families of 10 or 12 children were common in those days of often difficult rural life, when premature deaths were expected and children could provide labour to lift living standards for the entire family. Sarah and Samuel had a modest family of five, a daughter and four sons. My grandfather, Robert, the third son, was born on 11 June 1887, which indicates the family arrived quickly after the marriage. Perhaps that was just as well because, 10 years later, on 15 April 1897, my great grandfather was dead. He was only 41.

In the 19 years since his arrival in New Zealand Samuel had achieved a great deal. He had immersed himself in his new land. He and his new family looked

My great-grandfather's livery stables in Wyndham were behind the offices of the local newspaper. He must have had friends there because they wrote a wonderful obituary when he died.

ahead, they did not look back. That came at a cost to the past. In a forlorn letter written to Samuel on Christmas Eve two years before my great grandfather died, his own father had written:

"Dear Samuel, we are glad to hear from you once again, though we have written often and got no reply. We are all in fairly good health, except Mother, and she is very poorly. She can walk scarcely any and her health is failing her too. She feels deeply thankful to you for your kind present.

"We are glad to hear of you having been allowed to be so prosperous, hoping that you, Mrs and family are well."

Samuel's father and mother well knew the suffering of being left behind, their family scattered. The letter continued: "We get no word from any of the others except Charles. James is in Ballymena, working at his trade. John is in America and went to see Robert there, but did not remain with him. They never write, some of the neighbours mention them in their letters." Another brother, William, had also made his way to Wyndham but he had not stayed and Samuel, for many years, had had no idea of his whereabouts.

Perhaps they had a premonition but, shortly before his death, what the local newspaper described as the "numerous friends" of Samuel Richardson had gathered at Wyndham's Leahy's Hotel for a formal "presentation." In song and speech the town's business leaders praised him, his family and his business for what they had brought to Wyndham. Great-Grandfather received an "extremely handsome" silver tea and coffee service of four pieces, suitably inscribed. Guests were called upon to "charge their glasses and drink bumpers to the health and prosperity of Mr and Mrs Richardson."

"The toast was vociferously drunk with musical honours," the newspaper reported. "Mr Richardson, who was evidently considerably embarrassed, replied. He thanked them heartily on behalf of his wife and for himself. He had simply thought he was doing his duty and nothing more." The only doubtful note of the night was a song by one Mr Davey which the newspaper reporter thought, "with better taste, might have been omitted."

His death was dramatically reported: "Although it was generally known throughout the community that Mr Samuel Richardson had been confined to his bed since Friday last, the news of his death at a few minutes past seven o'clock yesterday morning came as a totally unexpected event." Two doctors, one of whom had travelled by train from Invercargill, attended him without success.

"The deceased gradually sank, however, and breathed his last at the hour already stated. The medical certificate ascribes the cause of death to exhaustion of the system – cardiac syncope," the newspaper said, before adding mysteriously: "It is said that certain reflections which Mr Richardson considered had been made upon his good name had caused him much worry of late and had not conduced to the welfare of a sensitive temperament nor of a constitution which for some years had been anything but robust."

The Mataura Ensign's obituary contained great praise. "The late Mr Richardson was one of the most outstanding landmarks in the whole of the Mataura Valley," its reporter noted. "Taking no prominent part in public affairs, yet from his geniality, sterling character and goodness of heart, he commanded the warmest

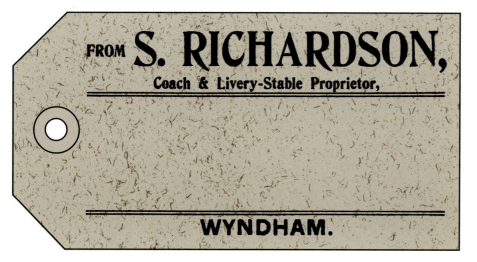

A well-preserved ticket that has long survived my great grandfather's business.

affection of legions of friends, not only in this district but in many other parts of the colony, and up to the day of his demise no more popular man than he stood in Southland.

"Evidences of the public appreciation of Poor Sam's worth were frequently forthcoming. An enemy of no man, the friend of hundreds, a personality the like of which has always tended to the betterment of humanity has disappeared from our midst and in our regret at the untimely cutting off of one who was in the highest sense of the word a model citizen and colonist, we offer to the bereaved ones, who are left to bewail the loss of husband and father, our sincerest sympathy and condolence in their great trial."

What links with Samuel's family remained after his death are unknown – only the week before they had learned from his father that his mother had died – but my great grandmother did not seem to spend a long period in mourning. The family memories are that she was resourceful. In the event she retained the business, in conjunction with her brother, William Cruickshank, who must have followed his sister to New Zealand. Her husband's death might even have inspired her because, on 26 July 1897 – not long after he died – Sarah saw an opportunity. She took up the lease on a hearse, complete with plumes, cover pole and harnesses, with the right to purchase for £100 after five years. The funeral business, however, can't have been an overwhelming success. When the lease ran out my great grandmother simply renewed it for another five years.

Sarah sold the business in 1911. She had run it well, under the watchful eye of brother William. Her family was growing up and her son William had also helped manage it. Much was changing. Initially the coaches had met the trains at Edendale and run south to Fortrose. Then the rail arrived in Wyndham, while the train to Waimahaka ended the necessity for a coach service to Fortrose. So the Richardsons had started services to other towns and districts unserved by rail, including Mataura Island and Wyndham Valley, and continued the goodwill started by Sam who refused to turn away customers simply because they didn't have the money to pay. As well, they continued his habit of providing free transport to the local district picnic.

None of the family obviously wanted to take over the business. Perhaps they had already astutely watched the arrival of the steam train and accurately predicted the advent of the internal combustion engine as the end of the horse transport business. Daughter Jane became Mrs Osborne Mackay and she and her husband were storekeepers in Wyndham. Archibald was an engineer who worked for the Atlantic Oil Company and was later a Wellington city councillor. After helping his mother and uncle run the stables and horses William became manager of the mercantile firm, National Mortgage in Wyndham, while George, regarded as the family tearaway, was a machine gunner in World War 1 and died at a young age.

Sarah also was honoured with a "presentation" by the good people of Wyndham when she quit the business and coverage of that event extended to one and a half columns in the newspaper. She was to live in her first home for 54 years until ill health forced her to move in with her daughter and husband. In 1936, she died at the age of 74. The business premises became the local garage.

Their other children had their successes, but it was Robert who would establish the family in commerce on a larger scale. He did not follow his parents into transporting both the living and the dead; nor could he have dreamed how the family's business would evolve. His parents had instilled in their children a sense of commerce when they ran their coach service. Robert was to look in other directions. Yet the principles remained the same. In business, as in life, it's a matter of taking opportunities.

My great grandmother, Sarah, was a stalwart woman who carried on the family business after her husband died.

2

ONE DAY I WAS STANDING IN THE POST OFFICE in Invercargill collecting the mail from our post box. Gathering his mail alongside was an older businessman whom I recognised. I greeted him by name.

"Who are you?" he asked.

"I'm Bill Richardson," I replied, to which he asked whether I was a son of Harold Richardson. I confirmed that I was.

He looked at me and said: "Your father wasn't a bad fellow. Your grandfather was a bastard."

You tend to remember statements like that. In my eyes, he was no such thing. Grandfather Robert was a kindly, gentle man with the gift of getting on well with children, just like his father had been at the Wyndham district picnics. Yet he was obviously no mug and he was to extend the family's business acumen in no small way.

Robert left school and was apprenticed to a builder in Wyndham called Samuel Shaw, who had been a carpenter before coming to New Zealand from, of all places, the county of Antrim, Northern Ireland. His first job was to build a small glasshouse which was still standing 60 years later. He was 25 when he married Letitia Linda Boyce in Cambridge on 17 April 1912. Why he had travelled such a distance is unclear but later accounts of his life were to say he wanted to further his career in the building industry and he saw opportunity there. Once married they travelled south, spending a year or so in Timaru where their first son, Douglas, was born. In the years following, they would raise seven children although one, Charles, would die at the age of four.

My grandfather, Robert, started work in Wyndham for Samuel Shaw, whose sign indicated he was prepared to try anything. In this picture, taken in 1907 when Grandad was about 20, Sam Shaw is pictured fifth from left by the single door and my grandfather is third from right.

Wyndham Dairy Factory was among my grandfather's building projects.

My grandfather takes his children for a ride in his Renault car in Wyndham.

In 1916, an opportunity arose. Samuel Shaw was aged 49 at a time when men often died young. He was a man deeply involved in civic affairs and he wanted to step out of his business and immerse himself more fully in community work. At the age of 29, Robert, or Bert as he was known by many, bought him out and continued the business. Throughout Wyndham, Otara, south-west towards Mokoreta, as the farmland of the area was more and more developed and the agricultural potential of the south grew, my grandfather worked hard building mainly residential dwellings.

It would be no exaggeration to say he was fairly successful with his business. He built the Wyndham Dairy Factory for a tendered price of £5091/3/5 ($10,182.35), and the Roman Catholic Church for £2659/10/- ($5319). Comparative prices of the day make fascinating reading. An obviously substantial house was built for £906/14/11 at Redan. My grandfather's margins were not huge. He estimated Wright Stephenson and Co's grain store at Edendale would cost £615/8/6, including labour of £80, and quoted £655 for the job. He costed a cow byre for £105/7/4, including labour of £12. His quote of £110 allowed him a profit of £4/13/8.

Yet he was not short of a few bob and he was not afraid to spend it. My father, Harold George Richardson, would later explain this was partly because of the free labour he and his brother, Bill, provided for their keep only. Just before the Depression in the 1930s, Grandad was able to buy a new De Soto, a very reasonable American car for the times. In 1933 he bought an International 18 cwt truck at a time when many people were cutting down old cars and turning them into trucks. In 1938, he bought a new Vauxhall. A year later he bought a new Diamond T truck, which was probably the most expensive truck he could have bought. As well he built himself a new home in Wyndham, which is still standing, with a nicely pointed brick fence of quite ornate design.

If my grandfather was a hard businessman it is not difficult to understand why. He took up the business during World War 1 when times were tough indeed and a generation of young men were dying on foreign battlefields, their sacrifices to be marked forever on countless war memorials in home towns like Wyndham and its surrounding districts. The cost of the war effort in human and economic terms was huge, and only the fittest or most necessary of businesses survived. The 1920s offered little respite and history well records how the world became unstuck at the end of that decade. Some might see my grandfather's survival as brutal capitalism, which it was. But his very survival when others, who in personality were far more brutal, fell apart, speaks volumes for his business skills. The fact that

Grandad with his daughter, Molly, and a pampered moggy.

The Richardson home at 38 Alice Street, Invercargill. My uncle Douglas's Morris 8 is parked outside.

State houses grew like mushrooms around the eastern suburbs of Invercargill.

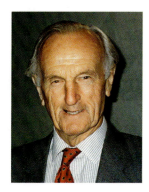

Uncle Sam was always good fun and still is to this day.

he had two sons who worked for him for their keep undoubtedly helped.

My father was another third son, born on 13 July 1915. He left school at the age of 13. There was no work for him immediately in his father's business and he was sent to Fortrose for a year to help relations milk cows. Grandfather Robert would never be out of work during the Depression but at one stage the only job on hand was making a picket fence.

When Dad was 18, and his brother Bill a year or two younger, my grandfather sent them as part of their apprenticeship to Venlaw Station to build a house for its owner, Colin Story. Venlaw Station was perhaps the major station of south-eastern Southland, a vast spread of land south-east of Wyndham. Having provided the plans and the materials, Grandad left them to it saying: "Get cracking and build the house."

My father looked at his brother and said: "What do we do now?" Uncle Bill replied: "Well, you're the oldest. You tell me what to do."

They set to and started to build. Obviously they were not without some knowledge. Yet they certainly struggled, even after they studied and re-studied the plans. Still, before the foothills of the magnificent station a house gradually rose from their foundations. Pitching the roof proved particularly difficult. Cutting the right angles proved almost impossible, so the two youngsters learned and built from experience. The ground was littered with incorrectly cut pieces of timber. Yet, as Shakespeare shrewdly noted centuries before, there was method in this madness.

Years later, not long before Grandad died, Bill asked a question that had long perplexed him: "The Story house that Harold and I built – you couldn't have made any money out of it?"

My grandfather looked at him and said: "No, I didn't make any money out of it. But I made two carpenters."

* * *

In 1935, 17 years into his own business, my grandfather was looking further afield than Wyndham and the surrounding districts. The Depression would have been among the reasons. This was a time when survival depended on being fit and fast. For decades Southland had suffered from inadequate hospital facilities and, in the 1930s, the Government acted. A new hospital would be built in the suburb of Kew.

My grandfather successfully tendered a price of about £19,000 for the laundry block, which consisted of a laundry and a large chimney. Having won the contract he had to think anew. Invercargill was some distance from Wyndham. The family would rent a house not far away from the project, but Grandad decided he needed a project manager. When a father owns the company and an intermediary is placed between the father and the worker sons, personalities have to jell.

They didn't. The brothers despised him. The project

manager had a leg defect and my father, Bill and the eldest son Douglas, three young fit men, teased him mercilessly. For his part he wanted them fired, but they were the boss's sons so they couldn't be sacked. It was a tense relationship. Once, when Bill was under a concrete floor with my father, stripping boxing, the project manager told them he wanted to see them. They both called out: "If you want to see us, come and get us, you old so and so." For all that the project manager appears to have been quite efficient, because that project led to others.

There was not much to the company's assets. At the time of the move into Invercargill plant consisted of the 18cwt International truck, shovels, spades, minor tools and two unused woodworking machines. Once the Kew Hospital job was secure a concrete mixer capable of mixing one third of a cubic yard at a time and a bar cutter were hired from a Dunedin construction company, and a winch bought from a Ministry of Works sale at the Waitaki hydro-electric scheme. As well it was time to buy an electric saw.

My father had learned his trade well. In fact he would not live in Wyndham again, and my grandfather began to rely on his construction abilities more and more. Invercargill was a city and therefore offered greater work opportunities, so a house was bought in Ness Street. After a while they bought 38 Alice Street, where Grandad lived until his death.

The Depression was still causing much misery and had highlighted some of the least desirable aspects of living in New Zealand for many people. Among them was housing. According to an official report, by the end of the 1930s there were some 27,000 houses urgently in need of demolition. Another 55,000 were in urgent need of repair.

Elected in 1935, the Labour Government of the time had embarked on a State housing scheme among other social welfare initiatives which were to last for the next 50 years. A Department of Housing Construction was formed, urged on by a Government whose zeal and audacity had to be admired. In three years some 3445 houses had been built throughout the country. Some of them were planned for the Tay, Islington, Millar and Tweed Streets area of East Invercargill.

Perhaps more significantly, the houses set new standards for construction and

The foundations are laid for the laundry block at Kew Hospital, the job that prompted my grandfather's shift from Wyndham to Invercargill.

The team that built the laundry block. My father is on the left in the fourth row from the front, Uncle Bill is sixth from right in the back row and Uncle Doug is second from right in the third row. Long term employee of the Firm, Joe Hayes, is second from left in the third row.

design, and the Government wasn't interested in being ripped off. This showed in the tendering process. Documentation included a schedule of quantities. That's common today but it wasn't then and many contractors shied away at having to be so precise. It held no such fears for my father and grandfather and they won the contract. In all they were to build 156 houses.

The company grew rapidly. Among other projects it built wool stores in Annan Street, a convent at Nightcaps, a miners' hostel at Ohai, the Sacred Heart Catholic Church at Waikiwi, St Patrick's Catholic Church at Georgetown and St Mary's Hall. My grandfather was a Protestant but the Catholic Church provided his company with a lot of work over the years. For good measure the company also built the Scottish Hall for a sternly Protestant organisation. The first job worth more than £100,000 was at the Gore Hospital.

They had standards and Grandad insisted on them. While setting out the boxing for the foundations of St Patrick's

My father and mother on their silver wedding anniversary.

Catholic Church my father and Uncle Bill discovered that part of the work was off square. They mentioned this to their father as they were sitting down to tea that night. My grandfather ordered them back to the job without finishing their meal. They found when remeasuring that the tape had been twisted and they had been reading the wrong side. It was square after all. Another mistake they didn't correct. The plans for one of the State houses were read upside down, and it was built back to front. It remained functional, but it wasn't how it was meant to be.

* * *

The years of the Second World War were tough. All materials were rationed and all building projects strictly monitored to ensure they were of the highest priority. Grandfather scored a considerable coup in 1941 when he won the tender to build Tweedsmuir Intermediate School in Tweed Street, Invercargill's first such school, for the large sum of £25,170 ($50,340).

With so many young men off at the war, finding and keeping staff was a nightmare. All staff on that particular job were "manpowered" to it. By Government decree they were forced to work on the project. As can be imagined this was by no means ideal for employee or employer. Workers were forced to be there, the boss was forced to take them on, regardless of their skills and abilities. A headline in the paper read: "Like Sword of Damocles hanging over you." It was a reference to awaiting the outcome of a manpower hearing about Dad and repeated a statement my grandfather had made. Some of those so "manpowered" to the job, however, were to stay with the company for many years.

In the 1950s, R Richardson Ltd, which had officially been formed in 1944, was to win another large contract at Tweedsmuir school, building the assembly hall. But, in his haste, my father forgot to include the cost of the roof in his tender. Those are the tenders you always win, and so we did, building the hall at a loss. Many years later a man arrived to hire one of our skips and I idly asked him what he wanted it for. The roof on Tweedsmuir's assembly hall was being replaced, he explained, and they needed the skip for the old tiles. The irony was delightful. My father put the roof on and didn't get paid, and we were getting paid to take it away.

Right: St Patrick's Catholic Church in Georgetown was to teach my father and uncle a stern lesson.

Below: Sacred Heart Catholic Church in Waikiwi was another R Richardson project.

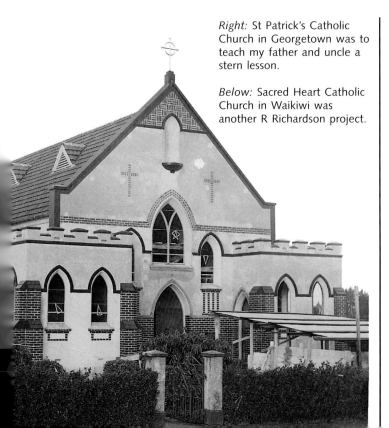

St Mary's Hall arises in Nith Street, Invercargill.

The company grew further, constructing many of the city's substantial buildings. Among the projects was the Peacehaven Old People's Home. That portion of southeast Invercargill could have been called Richardsonsville. Peacehaven was at one end, Tweedsmuir School at the other, and in between were State houses, all built by the firm. The Tisbury Dairy Factory, Kingslands biscuit factory and Southland Butchers By-Products abattoir at Waikiwi were among other projects. The last-named the company built twice. After it burned down we had another go at it.

There were numerous schools – Tisbury, Clifton, Limehills and Dacre, and extensions to Surrey Park and North. In the baby-booming years of the late 1950s, 1960s and early 1970s, as Invercargill grew and grew the company won the initial contracts at Rosedale Intermediate, Lithgow Intermediate, James Hargest High School, Kingswell High School, Cargill High School and Verdon College. As well we built the Glengarry Tavern, the Calvary Hospital, Clifton sewage treatment plant, the original Branxholme water treatment plant and a large water reservoir at Waikiwi. Major city projects included Phoenix House (now NZI House), the SIMU building, the Don Street police station, Karitane Hospital, Invercargill Airport terminal and railway locomotive sheds.

We were not afraid of change or innovation. The locomotive sheds consisted of a concrete building with a concrete roof, which was unusual for the time. The roof was to be poured on the ground and lifted into place. We won the job because Railways called tenders for two roof designs, the other being a conventional type of roof. Only Fletcher Construction and Richardsons tendered in the end and Fletchers, believing Railways would not proceed with the concrete roof, tendered only for a conventional roof. In the event Railways proceeded with the concrete roof and we won the job.

* * *

They were interesting, challenging years during which R Richardson Ltd established itself as one of the south's major building companies. But its list of achievement and construction tells only part of the story. The more important part of the story is a chronicle of struggle and survival, of business acumen and sheer stubbornness, gall and absolute cheek.

Both Grandad and my father were strong-minded men who knew how to do business. There were no pretensions about them. In the business sense they were close in that Dad worked for and closely with his father. But he was also very much his own person.

At the age of 23, in January 1939, he married Joyce Wensley. Joyce lived in Crinan Street and Dad lived in Ness Street not far away. Joyce worked in the lolly department of McKenzies department store, and Dad was smitten. I entered this world as Harold William Richardson on 17 October 1940. My brother Ken followed 17 months afterwards.

Our three generations of Richardsons were a typically hierarchical family of those times. My grandfather was undoubtedly the boss, which was perhaps just as well in their early days. My father could be somewhat hot-headed. On one wool store job he demanded that the clerk of works be replaced and walked off the job until he was. Today probably no builder would get away with that sort of behaviour. But as the years went by and I grew up my father exerted more and more control. My memory of my grandfather was that he worked behind the scenes.

However Grandad had a sideline interest that would eventually become synonymous with our name. It was called the Niagara Sawmilling Company, after the district in the extreme south of New Zealand. The company had two sawmills, one at Blackhorn in the Waikawa Valley and one at Progress Valley. It was far from successful.

Niagara Sawmilling had been formed in 1935 by a character called Jim Farrelly, a big Irishman whose great sense of humour was not matched by his management abilities. His company had come about only after a great deal of ill-feeling when Farrelly, while working for the Fortification Timber Company, started proceedings to form Niagara. Fortification directors took a dim view of this because Farrelly was their manager and also one of their shareholders. They sacked him. To compound those ill feelings he also took some of Fortification's customers with him, including my grandfather, who was building the Government houses at the time.

In 1936 Niagara, through Jim Farrelly, bought another sawmill, forming Standard Timber Company to do so. Then in 1939, the year that Grandad became a Niagara shareholder and director, with grudges momentarily forgotten, Niagara and Fortification formed Te Peka Timber Company,

R Richardson Ltd lifts the concrete roof on new railways sheds in Invercargill in 1963.

Niagara having a controlling 62.5 percent interest. Te Peka Timber established a large timber dressing plant at its namesake, near Waimahaka, to further process timber from both Fortification and Niagara's mills.

During those times timber was taken by road from Niagara's mills to Te Peka. Fortification's mill was closer to Te Peka and a steel railway was formed between the two. One of the tractor drivers on that run was the legendary Burt Munro, who became renowned for his world motorcycle racing and land speed record attempts, particularly in the United States. Munro was another character and Farrelly's brother-in-law as well. Stories abound of him riding his motor bike the full length of the veranda at the Waimahaka Store before leaping over the drop at the end. Being mechanically minded and speed mad he was also given to tuning the engines of the rail tractors to make them go faster. In theory this might have seemed sensible, the reality was that they often derailed.

Against such a tempestuous beginning it isn't surprising that animosities were not long in coming to the surface again and the joint venture fell apart after only three years. The arguments and bad feelings can be imagined. In the end, Fortification agreed to sell their shares to Niagara as long as Farrelly sold his shares in Fortification.

Around the Niagara board table, however, the arguing continued. Farrelly was a man whose character is best illustrated by the stories told about him. He would get himself into some dreadful scrapes, and nearly always managed to emerge unscathed. He was also unusual, something of a loner, with a wife in Invercargill, although he lived there only occasionally. Yet while living their separate lives they were a close couple.

His performance as a director and manager led to many disagreements. In 1945 he was actually asked to leave a board meeting while his unsatisfactory performance was discussed. Called back in, he was asked for his resignation and gave it. At the next meeting, the company's minutes record the appointment of a new manager. But that was the last to be heard of the new man. His name never appeared in the minutes again. Jim Farrelly just carried on as usual.

The way they did business was sometimes astounding. On one occasion they needed a new truck. They received a quote for a REO truck from T R Taylor in Invercargill and ordered it. Two months later directors met again. In the meantime, they had decided to look at three vehicles, the REO, a Studebaker and an International. A representative from Studebaker was asked to attend and, having received his quote, the directors decided to order a new Studebaker truck. At the next meeting the Chairman happily reported the company's new truck had been bought. It was an International. The pricing made less sense than the decision-making. The REO was to cost £976, the Studebaker £817 while the International eventually cost £985. Perhaps it was the £25 deposit and balance at £25 a month at an interest rate of 4.5 percent that swung the decision in a cash-strapped company. There was no further mention of the two trucks already ordered.

In the years after the war rumours of shortages were constantly heard. On one occasion Farrelly heard that axes were to be in short supply. He went to every hardware merchant he could find and bought all their axes. That meant finding storage for them. We had axes in our builders' store, Farrelly had axes in his house, and there were even axes in our truck garage at Tokanui because Farrelly hid them from his workers in case they wanted a new one when their old ones hadn't worn out.

He also had the gift of eloquence, as you'd expect from an Irishman. I recall, as a youngster, being in the bush one day and a hauler, used to pull logs out of the bush, had become stuck. Farrelly and his head bushman called Bert Murdoch had a heated argument on how to free the machine. Murdoch lost the argument with his boss and stormed off saying: "I wash my hands of the whole thing."

Top left: A Wilson Bros 3-71GM-powered 12-wheel-drive rail tractor hauls logs out of the bush at Niagara.
Left: The infrastructure required to get logs from the bush to the mill was extensive.

Farrelly did it his way and the hauler became unstuck. I can see him yet – a big man given to wearing a gaberdine overcoat, standing on a tree stump before the gathered workmen – calling out to Bert Murdoch: "Well, Pontius Pilate, are you satisfied now?"

The bushmen over the years were of all nationalities, among them White Russian refugees. Farrelly one night took them to an Invercargill butcher shop and was ordering meat and sausages for them. They greeted his generosity with cries of anguish. They waved their arms and yelled at him in Russian, to the point that Farrelly gave up. Only later did he discover they were confirmed vegetarians.

He attracted some committed staff around him, including a Scandinavian called Sodestrom. His nickname was Scandy and he was known to drink a lot. But he always stayed with Jim Farrelly.

Scandy lived in a hut in Progress Valley and once discovered a Scotsman stacking timber late one night.

"What are you doing, stacking timber in the dead of night?" he asked.

"I'm trying to help Mr Farrelly out," the Scotsman replied.

"What are you helping him out for?"

"I was talking to him this afternoon and he was telling me times are hard and he's losing a lot of money."

Scandy put him right: "I wouldn't take any notice of that. I've been working for that old bastard for 30 years and times have always been hard and he's been losing money. He must have lost millions and millions in the time I've been working for him."

Farrelly also promised his workers and their families things he couldn't deliver, either through lack of money or through his own lack of diligence.

It was obviously a day to celebrate when H E Melhop Ltd delivered a Leyland-powered rail tractor to Niagara Sawmilling Co. At left is H E Melhop himself while Jim Farrelly (wearing the hat) is pictured leaning on the log.

He promised two women baths for their houses and one day, on the Waikawa Freight, one tin bath duly arrived. Farrelly arrived in his car not long afterwards to find both women fighting over the bath. When they turned on him for failing to deliver he was unabashed.

"From what I can see, you're that grubby you'll never use it," he told one woman, before turning to the second: "You're that fat you'll never fit into it." He gave the tin bath to a third woman.

The battles around the Niagara board table were to have more than one beneficial effect for my family, however. In 1946, when Niagara had yet another financial crisis, directors decided to sell their two trucks to try to raise some capital. My father saw an opportunity and, in partnership with Alf Pearce, raised the £1800 ($3600) necessary to buy a 1936 International C40F and a 1938 International DS216T. Dad, with 55 percent of the shares, and Alf with 45 percent, formed Southern Transport that same year.

It was my father's first business and, in its early days, it was far from financially successful. Alf Pearce pulled out. Bruce Benneworth took his shares then he too pulled out. Harry Aitken was an old friend of my father and a partner in an electrical company called Parkinsons Ltd. In spite of the company's short and chequered history he was willing to become a partner. My father warned him he might lose his money but Harry replied: "If you're game, I'm game."

3

IN 1948 MY FATHER'S TIME CAME. He bought R Richardson Ltd. My grandfather was 61. It was time to retire, although not before he decided he and his wife would travel to England and Ireland.

At one stage R Richardson Ltd was the largest client of Briscoes, international hardware merchants, in Australasia. Grandad naturally needed transport in the United Kingdom and thought a prestigious 1.5 litre Jaguar would do the trick nicely. He charged it to the Briscoes account, leaving it to others to sort out the details of how this arrangement would be confirmed and financed. He and my grandmother toured England and Ireland, sold the Jaguar and then came home. Among the things he did overseas was look up some family members in Ireland.

There was no room for sentimentality in handing on the business from one generation to the next. My father believed the business was worth £4000 ($8000). Grandad wanted £6000. The arguments began. My father claimed it wasn't worth £6000 because he believed he had created any goodwill in the business. My grandfather stuck firm and my father found the £6000.

But what Grandad hadn't told him was that the company owed unpaid taxes of £4000, which meant it cost my father £10,000. Fortunately the Inland Revenue Department took a benevolent view and allowed him time to pay.

This did nothing for family unity but my father was ready for the challenges ahead. He was a naturally aggressive man and good fortune had largely smiled upon him. Our first family house was in Tramway Road, Invercargill, built in 1938 and 1939, but Dad then built a pleasant, pointed brick house in Swinton Street. It had hardly been finished when there was a knock on the door one Saturday. A real estate agent stood there, saying his clients were three spinster sisters from Bluff looking for a house in the city. They liked ours.

My father replied that it was not for sale. The agent persisted. The sisters would pay good money. Dad repeated it was not for sale. The agent said it was worth about £800. Dad repeated: It was not for sale.

My father in his own yard and running his own business.

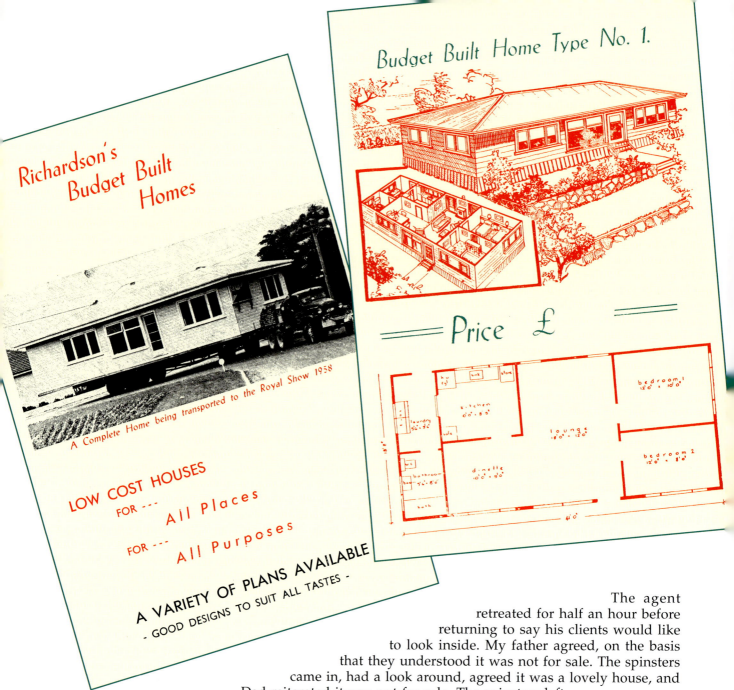

A pamphlet told of the benefits of buying a prefabricated house from R Richardson Ltd.

The agent retreated for half an hour before returning to say his clients would like to look inside. My father agreed, on the basis that they understood it was not for sale. The spinsters came in, had a look around, agreed it was a lovely house, and Dad reiterated it was not for sale. The spinsters left.

Thirty minutes later, the agent returned. "Look," he said, "we're still out there, they just want to buy it. Put a price on it."

"Two thousand pounds," exclaimed my father, thinking that exorbitant amount would choke them off. Five minutes later, the agent was back, beaming: "Sold!" So we moved out to a house in Wellington Street and he started building the house in Inglewood Road which is now my house.

There was logic to moving to this south-eastern part of Invercargill on the outskirts of the city. In 1944 my father had started a joinery factory in Anglem Street, which was parallel to Inglewood Road. This diversification was typically Richardson. The company was building Tisbury School and my father decided to make his own window frames. This caused considerable consternation to local joiners who obviously operated a nice cartel. If he did that, they said, they would not supply the flush doors.

That was a foolish threat to make to my father. He promptly went to Checketts Engineering, and asked them to build a press with which he could make his own flush doors. Having gone to that much trouble he decided he might as well be in the joinery business. My grandfather had not been so convinced at the time but Dad's will prevailed. A few years later Richardsons entered the fibrous plaster business through a similar experience. Building demand was high and local fibrous plaster suppliers were too slow in my father's view. So he went into fibrous plaster manufacturing. We also manufactured concrete roofing tiles for a short time.

The business grew and we took on more and more staff. We also became involved with plumbing and later painting, although the latter taught us a lesson – we needed to have tight controls. A woman contacted my father one day to complain about the quality of the painting the company had undertaken. Dad couldn't recall the job. An investigation revealed we had supplied the painters and the paint but the manager of the painting division had charged out the job and taken the money. His career with us was abruptly ended.

The company had some rather large painting projects, including Southland Girls' High School and the Civic Theatre and at our peak we employed between 15 and 17 painters. But we never made any money out of painting.

Fortunately, when Dad started on his own, good fortune smiled on what would today be called the core business. The Government announced a scheme to give better housing to sawmill workers, subsidising the building of houses. R Richardson Ltd tendered for 24 such houses, 12 for Blackhorn and 12 for Progress Valley mills, which were owned by Niagara Sawmilling Company at the time. The company won the contract. Again it showed innovation because the houses were built in Invercargill as prefabricated units which broke down into four separate pieces. Three of those pieces fitted on a six-wheel truck while a spare room and fourth piece fitted on a five-ton truck.

These were the days of stifled competition. Tokanui was 36 miles from Invercargill and the laws of the land were that you couldn't compete with New Zealand Railways beyond 30 miles. That meant carting timber destined for Invercargill by truck to the railhead and having it taken by rail from there to Invercargill. But the houses were, of course, far too large for rail wagons. Southern Transport's vehicles therefore carted the houses that R Richardson built to the mills and could cart timber back to the rail. It should be remembered that, in those days, timber had to be handled one stick at a time.

Sometimes our trucks did not stop there and continued on to Invercargill with their loads. The local station master was a vigilant man and, whenever he noticed such unlawful activity, he reported the company to the then equivalent of the Ministry of Transport, which prosecuted Richardsons with zeal. If my father's companies had managed what in today's terms is a double whammy by building the houses and carting them to their sites, the law also had a similar achievement in punishing errant transport companies. Not only did Southern Transport have to pay the fines, it also had to pay New Zealand Railways the freight charges it would have received had they carried the load.

Still, the contract gave Southern Transport reasonable continuity of work and by early 1949 the two old International trucks and an ex-Army GMC had been replaced with two new Ford Thorntons, which were Canadian Ford V8 tandem trucks. R Richardson Ltd bought a similar, five-ton truck and the two businesses began to cog together nicely.

Dad's Mercury car leads the way through the Chaslands as part of a prefabricated house is taken to its destination.

Not every prefabricated house journey went smoothly.
1) Part of the house is loaded on to the truck.
2) Truck hits pole, house falls off truck.
3) House is put back on truck, but not in our recommended condition.

I suspect my father made quite a lot of money in those days. Most significantly, this was the start of prefabricated housing, whereby houses could be built on a central site using many common elements. Staff became highly experienced in specific aspects of the job and economies flowed. From this would develop an aspect of housing construction for which Richardsons would become well known.

Richardsons offered "Budget Built" homes of what were described as "compact, practical design." They contained most items you'd find in a house and owners could choose their own colour schemes. They were built of red pine bearers and floor joists and totara or matai sills and were ready to connect to services. We offered free delivery within eight miles, as long as there was reasonable access to the site. After that it was 30 shillings a mile. A deposit of £100 to £300 was required, depending on the type of house, and two-thirds of the balance was required on delivery to the site. The rest had to be paid within 30 days.

In a fast-developing city and province, they were quick, comfortable and convenient and therefore very popular.

The company's premises became a prominent business landmark in Invercargill. Dad had bought sections in Anglem Street and the joinery factory and the various divisions just grew there – a store, plumbers' shop, the paint shop and the fibrous plaster manufacturing division, as well as an engineering division in the early 1950s to maintain the company's equipment. It was also, of course, a timber yard and that required heavy wood-working machinery. The building of the transportable homes resulted in a large builders' yard being created as well.

Initially the property was in Southland County but as Invercargill grew it became part of the city. The city council, however, wanted the land zoned residential, which would have caused us to move. Dad fought his first major battle with the council when he tried to establish the fibrous plaster manufacturing business. The council did not want him to build for that purpose. Dad persisted, and won. That turned out to be the rock the council foundered on because, later, when council pressure grew to have the entire block zoned residential, he was able to say the council had granted him a permit. In the end, the entire block was zoned commercial but Richardsons had to quit some properties on the other side of Anglem Street which then became residential. Our Anglem Street site just grew busier and busier.

* * *

Some old workhorses at rest before our new house in Inglewood Road by the headquarters of R Richardson Ltd. From left, they are the GMC 6 x 6, the International DS216T and the International C40F. The last two have been restored and are in my truck museum.

Dad was a restless man. He also wanted to try farming, a reflection perhaps of his Irish ancestry. He told us he was looking for a little farmlet somewhere handy to the city. One day my mother pointed out an advertisement in a newspaper for the sale of a 943-acre farm at Te Peka, 31 miles from Invercargill. Curious, because it was well placed for his wishes, and with our history in the area, Dad went to look at it and discovered he was sixth or seventh in line.

All ahead of him were established farmers. All, however, turned it down. One Sunday, Dad, Mum, Ken and I drove to the farm in our 1947 Mercury to see Henderson Holms, who was handling the sale. Dad had said he would turn the farm down as well and we sat in the car outside the gate as my father went in – we presumed to tell Holms he wasn't interested.

We waited and waited until, about an hour and a half later, Dad returned to tell us he had changed his mind. He had done a deal with Holms, a well-known Hereford cattle stud breeder. He would buy the farm for £5 an acre, pay £2000 deposit and, as soon as he put a house on it, the Holms family would give him back £1000 and have the balance as preferential shares in R Richardson Ltd.

There was logic in buying a scruffy piece of land consisting of three large paddocks and not a building to be seen. The war was over and New Zealand had a guaranteed market for its agricultural products in Great Britain, which would take as much as New Zealand could produce. Further, the outbreak of the Korean War had led to skyrocketing prices for wool. All over Southland, which was acknowledged as one of the agriculturally rich areas of New Zealand, vast tracts of land were being broken in.

We also found there was a misconception about the farm itself. Previous prospective buyers had turned it down because of a large hill running through the farm's centre, which they believed would be too steep to work. As it turned out, David Brown crawlers could plough the hill and slopes with comparative ease.

We took over the farm in April 1951 when I was 10. We cleared the gorse, matagouri scrub and tussocks and it became a very good farm indeed. Dad spent a lot of time on the property, and a lot of money as well.

In 1953 the Queen visited Invercargill and R Richardson Ltd entered this majestic float in the royal parade.

Down on the farm with its manager, George Stuart, and my brother Ken in a David Brown Cropmaster and Dad in a David Brown Trackmaster.

That was the year my grandfather died. I still remember him kindly. The art of writing obituaries seemed to have faded by the time of his death. The notice in the newspaper consisted of four paragraphs, and his name was misspelled once. The newspaper noted briefly his building interests, before adding he was an enthusiastic supporter of rugby, cricket and athletics.

Among the mourners was his old friend Jim Farrelly who went to 38 Alice Street to pay his last respects. My grandmother asked him: "Would you like to see Bert, Jim?"

Farrelly was taken through to the front bedroom where Grandad was lying in his coffin. With barely a glance at his old friend, Farrelly rubbed his hand along the side of the coffin and said: "My God, Bert, that's a beautiful bit of red pine they've put you in."

After Grandad's death my grandmother moved to Auckland where she died in 1965.

* * *

In 1954 another opportunity arose. Niagara Sawmilling Company was perhaps an obvious target, given the family connection and the way it could work in with Dad's other companies. Jim Farrelly was still there, and he agreed to sell, as did the widow of Harry Aitken, the manager of Briscoes Hardware Merchants (and no relation of his former transport partner). Grandad had owned the rest of the shares and when he died he bequeathed them to other members of his family, but not Dad, thanks to bad feelings related to selling the business which continued to the end.

My father was keen to buy the whole company and the other family members were keen to sell the shares because it was in financial difficulties. It cost Dad about £54,000 ($108,000) and he borrowed virtually all of it.

There must have been times early in his ownership when he wondered why he had bothered. He had two sawmills, both steam-driven and inefficient, and expensive to run, as were the bush haulers. He had one petrol-driven and three diesel-driven rail tractors. He discovered the precarious state of his tramlines quickly when the Progress Valley tramline was officially condemned. It contained 30 wooden bridges, all made from untreated red pine which had rotted due to poor maintenance because the previous owners were short of cash.

In the first two or three years under my father's control the company lost £25,000. At the same time it had expanded, taking up a block of bush at Mokoreta, behind Wyndham, where we were building a new sawmill. Dad had to build a very steep road into the bush there while the condemned Progress Valley tramline meant he had to build another road of about 3.5 miles into the bush just to get to the areas his men had been working. It was a major operation, especially when there was no

The yard of R Richardson Ltd grew busier and busier, and somewhat cramped when we brought the trucks in for a snapshot.

A Thames Trader with our HD5 Allis Chalmers bulldozer on the back. My father and the franchise holder had some arguments about that truck.

money and not much equipment.

Further, while Dad was spending time sorting out those problems on site he wasn't spending the time required in the building business. Inefficiencies crept in through the lack of hands-on management for a company with between 130 and 140 staff.

Our administration was shocking. We just never seemed to be able to get organised. It didn't help that Dad hated the office in Anglem Street and didn't want to spend time there. He preferred to work himself day and night. During the day he built sawmills and the like. At night he sat down to price contracts to keep the building business going.

We had a terrible record for not paying our bills because we didn't know where we were financially. We had borrowed up to the hilt, and we were undercapitalised. Sapping our profits were Niagara Sawmilling operations and 943 acres of farm. More than once the companies came close to financial collapse. But my father had a grand ability to retain the confidence of both his bankers and his creditors.

He was also lucky. In the mid to late 1950s, when we were going through our worst financial crisis, we were struggling to buy gear. Niagara had a five-year-old Cletrac bulldozer which had done a lot of work when we bought the company. We needed more heavy gear and bought an HD5 Allis Chalmers bulldozer from Andrews and Beavan and a Hanomag crawler from Melhops, which proved to be a disaster. Our Ford Thornton trucks had seen better days but we didn't have the money to replace them. The state of our trucks, however, was noted by Vernon Russell, who owned VTR Motors.

"You need new trucks," Vernon Russell told my father in January 1957. "I can sell you a Commer Diesel."

"I haven't got any money," Dad replied.

"Name your terms," offered Russell.

Those were dangerous words to say to my father.

"Okay, give us the truck now. I make the final payment on the Allis bulldozer in October. I can give you some money for it then."

The deal was made and we had a new truck. I was to drive it myself when I left school, carting timber from Mokoreta to Invercargill. In 1958 we bought a Thames Trader Diesel as well. Both vehicles had mechanical problems but, in spite of that, they were a vast improvement on what we had had. The better equipment allowed the company to get going again and gradually we built up our gear.

But the extent of our problems was well illustrated by our involvement with

Our Diamond T truck was something of a family favourite.

Noel McGregor, of Mt Linton Station. The station in Western Southland was one of the largest in the country and Noel McGregor was an enterprising, interesting man whose work in developing the station became quite legendary. In 1954 we placed eight prefabricated houses on the station as well as other work – roofing in the sheepyards, an innovation for the time, and a lot of work on the homestead.

On one visit, McGregor said to Dad: "How do you get on for money?"

"As a matter of fact, I'm a bit hard up," my father replied, explaining how his expansion had caused financial difficulties.

My father's luck was running true to form. "I've always been interested in looking for a Southland-based company that's not farming-based," McGregor asked. "Would you be interested in us buying some shares?" After serious consideration, my father and McGregor did a deal whereby he bought a third of R Richardson (which included Southern Transport and all of its three trucks and Niagara Sawmilling) for £20,000. McGregor paid with two cheques, one from the station and one from his children's family trust. I can still remember my father bringing home those two £10,000 cheques and handing them to me, saying: "You will never hold that much money in your hand again."

But it was only a temporary respite and the struggle continued. Noel McGregor was only in the company for four years before he died in tragic circumstances in 1958. Dad's relationship with his widow, who remarried, was not so harmonious and we eventually bought them out in 1964, 10 years after Noel McGregor had made his offer.

There were always difficulties. Macaulay Motors was a well-established Invercargill firm from which we had bought two Thames Trader trucks, which were British-built Fords. They were causing mechanical troubles and we argued with the company over who should pay. We believed the trucks were at fault, Macaulays believed we were to blame and the disagreement reached such a level that the manager, Bob Macaulay, came to our premises.

"You have a short memory," Macaulay told my father. "We've kept you in motor cars." Those were the days when new cars were hard to come by and dealers were arrogant enough to believe they were doing you a favour to let you buy one.

"I was always under the impression I'd paid for them," Dad replied.

That remark obviously prompted Macaulay's memory.

"You're years late paying your accounts," he exclaimed.

My father responded mildly: "Never more than 10 months."

* * *

Yet for all those firms who understandably cut off our credit, or refused to deal with us, there were quite a few who had a lot of faith in my father and the companies. He had an ability to get on well with people and he was always up-front with his creditors, something he taught me to do. If there's a problem, talk to your creditors. Don't make them chase you to find out what is going on.

Some companies were very lenient when we were up against it, like Southland Sand and Gravel, an Invercargill company. Caltex Oil was also accommodating, freezing our overdue account and allowing us to pay it off interest-free over time as long as we continued to keep our current account up to date. We were also looked after by Briscoes.

One day Dad received a cheque in the mail from Mac McIvor, of Georgeson Bros, joiners. It was for £1000, a considerable sum in those days. Dad was puzzled because Georgesons didn't owe us the money. He telephoned Mac.

"What's this cheque for £1000 for?"

"That's for timber I will buy off you one day," Mac replied. He knew we were in trouble, and he did that twice. Eventually, of course, he got the timber, but he helped us keep going in the meantime.

We remembered such people when we reached the stage of being able to pay our accounts and rewarded them in our future dealings for their help, understanding and co-operation when we were in trouble. It's a philosophy I still maintain.

*   *   *

One of the facts of life about living in Southland or other provinces is that those living there need to try to support themselves. About this time Dad became involved in the Southland Cement Company, which grew out of the Clifden Lime Company. Dad supported the company for purely parochial reasons. During the 1950s, while the Roxburgh hydro-electric power scheme was being built, Southland builders were starved of cement. Milburn, the only cement supplier in the area and based in Dunedin, couldn't supply the local market and the hydro scheme and left the local market to whistle. To say it caused ill-feeling was an understatement.

We bought cement from Belgium and China and it was usually a struggle to get enough. We were bigger than most builders and needed more. My father deeply resented the fact that as soon as the Roxburgh scheme started loyal customers were almost forgotten, the assumption being they would still be there when it was finished.

So the idea of making cement from lime at Orawia was born through some local enthusiasm from the Clifden Lime Company and Fletcher Construction. Fletchers built it and Dad was an immediate supporter. Unfortunately the kiln was a vertical one which was evidently cheaper in terms of construction but it made consistency of product extremely difficult. Consistency of cement strength, as I was to discover many years later when we entered the readymix concrete business, was paramount. Southland Cement Company had a lot of difficulty getting consistency correct.

Their problems were compounded in the late 1950s when the Roxburgh

The Glengarry Tavern: Pick the wall made of Southland cement.

scheme was winding down and Milburn decided to meet the new threat in the south. It kept the price of cement down and increased its supply to the south, generally making things as difficult as it could. The Southland Cement Company was soon in financial difficulties. A board room coup followed and my father became a director. Their first priority was to improve the lime-works' operation. It had been allowed to run down, yet it actually made money. Then they tried to fix the cement works.

The consistency problems were well known and when we won the contract to build the Glengarry Tavern Lloyd Raines, the Trust's general manager, specified that no Southland cement could be used on the project. Dad, being Dad, built two walls at the tavern, one with Milburn cement and the other with Southland. Perhaps inevitably, the Licensing Trust found out and a site meeting was called. Demolish the wall made of Southland cement, Dad was told, and rebuild it with Milburn.

"Which one is it?" asked the engineer.

"You're the expert who knows it's no good," Dad replied. "You tell me."

The engineer pointed to one. Dad said it was the other. (It wouldn't have mattered which one was chosen; my father would have indicated the other). Today, the Glengarry Tavern is still standing, one wall made from Milburn cement, the other made from Southland.

That was perhaps a typical example of a province not supporting its own product. Its largest sales were and always had been in Canterbury. But to survive, Southland Cement needed to raise its prices. It couldn't while Milburn held its prices down. Eventually, the Clifden company had only one option. Milburn bought it and closed it down. The price of cement, I remember, went up immediately.

4

MY FATHER was undoubtedly the biggest influence in my life. He was born to run a business and he wanted that to continue with later Richardson generations. From very early ages he involved Ken and me in what he was doing and we hung on his every word. After school and during the holidays, he took us with him everywhere. He talked about the business with us constantly, and there were no secrets. Our business was part of the household conversation.

I recall coming home from primary school one day and asking Mum: "How did Dad get on with the banker?" I knew he was going to the bank and that the company was under financial pressure.

My mother was very protective of us and we were brought up a very close family. Our life revolved around our business. Ken and I would come home from school, put on our overalls, fill our pockets with wine biscuits and down to the yard we would go. If Dad was there we would go wherever he was going. If he wasn't there we went with Snowy Kidd.

Snowy started working for Dad when I was six and he was with us for 17 years. He was Richardson's main driver, behind the wheel of a five-ton 1949 Ford. He would go out of his way to take us with him after school.

"You not away yet, Snow?" Dad would say as some load waited.

"Well, the boys will be home from school in a minute," Snowy would reply. "I thought they might like to come."

Naturally we went with him at every opportunity and Snowy became quite an influence on our lives. He is now 89 and still comes by quite regularly to say hello, especially for the Christmas break-up when he can look over the trucks. He was one of only two drivers allowed to have us in the cab. The other was Jim Guildford who drove one of the Tokanui trucks. We loved going with Jim during school holidays to help shift houses.

Dad was reasonably interested in trucks; otherwise he wouldn't have established Southern Transport. From him, I believe, I gained my fascination for vehicles and machinery. Dad's interest with them extended to a very good drawing of Grandad's Diamond T truck and developed further when he made a large 3ft model of one for

Ken and I had two driver mentors. Snowy Kidd would wait until we were home from school to give us rides in trucks.

Ken and me to play with. I've still got its tractor unit and it's been through a couple of generations in the meantime.

As a youngster my interest just kept on growing. The likes of Snowy and Jim took the time to encourage us. We always went to interesting places and it wasn't surprising my curiosity blossomed into a passion.

I had been collecting truck brochures from the age of eight, admiring the pictures and poring over the details. Dad initially would write away to truck distributors for me but, when I grew older, I did so myself, and I still have my collection.

Jim McGoldrick ran the Southland Carrying Company, which had a fleet of not-so-good Thornycroft trucks in Spey Street. Jim was a kindly old man, perhaps not a particularly good businessman, and I used to hang around his depot when I was 12 or so. He would always take the time to talk to me about trucks and to show me magazines and brochures.

Charlie Emerson, an Invercargill contractor who had torn up the tramlines of the city when trams ceased operations, provided more excitement. Charlie did a lot of excavation work for the City Council during the road rebuilding programme in the early to mid-1950s. He had several D4 traxcavators and, if I wasn't down at the yard after school, I was on my bike to wherever Charlie was working around the streets of East Invercargill. Like Jim McGoldrick, he always took the time to talk to me.

Uncle Sam, my father's brother, also influenced me to a large degree. He was the one who always took time with us kids. When Uncle Sam was around there was always fun to be had. He was a most impractical person, but he could laugh at himself. He also had a softer nature than other members of the family and he changed my outlook on caring for others and finding out what makes people tick. He is now 79 and lives in the North Island. I see him quite often and I still value his friendship greatly.

Kids always remember when they grow up the people who spend time with them and that's why I always try to take time with youngsters who show an interest today.

My years at Surrey Park Primary School and Tweedsmuir Intermediate School passed quickly and happily in a secure environment. My interest in trucks did not abate while attending Southland Boys' High School.

I failed School Certificate. My mother wanted me to return to try again but Dad was opposed.

"What you need to learn you won't learn at school," he said.

So I left school at the age of 16 and started work in 1957 to serve my time as a carpenter and joiner. We were never forced to go into the business but we never thought of doing anything else. It was only a matter of when.

Jim Guildford was another driver who was very good to Ken (centre) and me.

Father and two sons, all in the family business.

My three years in the joinery factory were most enjoyable. Tom Roberts was my first boss and his brother Ted was foreman. They too had a huge influence on me. They both had a keen sense of humour, which I think rubbed off on me. I always thank them for making me appreciate the humour in life.

* * *

One aspect became no laughing matter, however. In May 1960, as we continued to expand and expand and Dad continued to run the business as he always had, he suffered a brain haemorrhage. He had been to the doctor the week before to be told he had dangerously high blood pressure and to come back in a week to get some pills. He didn't last the week. Getting into bed one night he passed out.

My mother called the doctor who came to our home. "I think he has ricked his neck. Take this note and get it X-rayed in the morning at Kew Hospital," the doctor advised. In the morning, he was still unconscious. My mother again called the doctor, who decided he'd better get a second opinion. Consequently, I didn't have much faith in that doctor.

My father was only 45, at what should have been the peak of his business life. Instead he had been struck down by serious illness only 12 years after he had taken over the business. His illness thrust me, at the age of 19 and just over halfway through my apprenticeship, into being much more involved in the management of the company. We had an accountant but I had to learn quickly the practical things like helping to buy supplies for the mills and building contracts, and how to help keep our transport and logging equipment going so that, in turn, we kept the company going. It didn't take long to learn that our administration was a shambles and that there was no natural chain of command. Various people ran bits of the company but nobody controlled the overall business.

Dad's illness had coincided with an extremely busy time. We were building State flats in Lithgow Place, Yarrow Street and Lyon Street, State houses in Lithgow Street, and quite a few commercial buildings. We had jobs all over the city.

It also coincided with probably the most important decision of my business life. By the time Dad returned to work later in 1960, Ken was working through his apprenticeship and I found I had a confession to make. I didn't want to be a builder.

"What do you want to do?" Dad asked.

"I want to run trucks," I said.

"You'll never get in a big way running trucks," he said.

"Maybe not, but that's what I want to do," I replied.

37

"Well," my father said, "I've always done what I wanted to do, so you'd better do what you want to do." And that was that. Mind you, Dad probably had whetted my appetite further in 1958 when he took Ken and me to the North Island, the first time we had been there. We saw trucks, loggers and other equipment on a scale far larger than anything we were used to and the idea grew in my mind that I wanted to be in that industry.

Transport was still a heavily licensed industry in 1960. It wasn't simply a case of buying a truck and hanging out a shingle. There were only a limited number of licences available, and a newcomer wanting to break into the industry had to buy an existing licensed operation. The company's transport business, Southern Transport, wasn't licensed to be a general carrier. It only had licences to cart timber for Niagara Sawmilling.

The presumption had been that I would go out on my own but Dad mulled over what I had said and one day came to me.

"If we bought a small one-truck business to get a general goods licence and attached it to Southern Transport would you stay with the family firm?" he asked.

"Yes, I would," I replied.

What seemed a happy compromise was not initially easy to achieve. We couldn't find such a one-truck business. So we raised our sights slightly and bought a business called South Invercargill Transport Company, which had four trucks – two seven-ton Karrier trucks, a five-ton Commer and a five-ton A5 Bedford – and three vehicle authorities, one of which was required for each vehicle under a Goods Service Licence. Owned for eight years by Jim Collett and Eric Kerr, the trucks worked around Waimatua, Tisbury, Clifton, Greenhills and other areas close to South Invercargill.

The price was just £8900 and we borrowed all the money from the Caltex Oil Company. This was easy to do in those times, particularly if the company being bought purchased its fuel from a rival oil company. In our case Caltex provided the money and increased its business share as a result. BP lost a customer.

South Invercargill Transport was hard up and the old Commer was shot. My vague memory is that the owners were selling because they had to pay back the money they had borrowed to buy the company. They hadn't made an awful lot of progress in the eight years. But we tidied up the fleet, painting the trucks cream and green. The painter dismissed for dishonesty had settled on those colours some time before and our painters had been enthusiastic. Even the plough on the farm was cream and green and in the initial plant store in Anglem Street wheelbarrows, scaffolding, ladders . . . everything was cream and green. When we bought a seven-ton Commer truck, which I had to collect from Greymouth just before Christmas – it had been shipped there for some unknown reason – it too became cream and green. From a single-purpose trucking concern, Southern Transport was in the much-larger general and rural carrying business, continuing the rural-type work we inherited in the Waimatua and Tisbury areas.

I soon discovered I knew very little about transport. But Dad was unsympathetic. He told me it was my business and I had to run it. He didn't want anything to do with it, even though it was part of the family business and Dad was its head. In

Our Southern Transport fleet in 1961, which also included our first purchase, South Invercargill Transport.

today's terms he would be considered group chief executive and chairman of the board but we were never that formal. Yet, looking back, I'm grateful that he stated his position so clearly because I had to learn by myself and then I had to learn how to stay ahead.

We bought another Commer and a Leyland Super Comet, our third diesel. I already knew and rapidly had reconfirmed that trucks could be contrary pieces of equipment. Our mechanical troubles continued with the three diesels. Frankly, we grew sick of diesels and, in November 1961, bought an International AACO182 with a petrol engine. We went International because it was the only company which would give us a trade-in on the Thames Trader. The salesman was Ron Scherp and 38 years later we would still be buying trucks from him. But there was still a lot to be learned and what makes truck sense one day makes little sense the next.

* * *

I began in the trucking business on my own at the age of 20, working out of Richardson's Anglem Street headquarters, but good advice came from unexpected sources. I was living at home in Inglewood Road and one day I walked out of our gate when an elderly man stopped beside me. I recognised him as Dave King, of D T King Ltd, a large, well-established trucking company which used to shift our prefabricated houses for us.

"They tell me you've bought a carrying business, lad," he said.

"That's right, Mr King," I replied.

"Well, you won't make any money out of it," he said.

"Why's that?" I asked.

"You're too close to town," the old man, who lived nearby, offered. "All those farms you're servicing are close to the fertiliser works, close to the freezing works, close to the lime works. You're not going anywhere. You need to get back a bit where you'll get decent, longer carts."

In that piece of advice he proved to be dead right. But he continued: "You want to keep an eye on those drivers. You'll find they don't care if the back wheels are falling off as long as the seat under their backsides is comfortable." That piece of advice always amused me.

* * *

For three years we plugged away in transport, performing reasonably while the family business went through its ups and downs. In business you have no choice but to keep going. I may have been the manager but it was hands-on all the way. I also drove trucks when needed.

A new opportunity arose in November 1963 when we bought Kennington Transport from Lex Turnbull. It had quite a history, having been owned at various times by Stan Cloughley, Fred Walker and Alan North. We paid £14,000 for the company, the operations side of which consisted of an AA 164 International and three S Bedfords. But in what would later turn out to

This photograph is of an earlier fleet of Kennington Transport than the one we bought, but is taken on the site of the present Kennington sawmill.

Shona and me on our wedding day in April 1965.

be a highly significant purchase for the family business the deal included an old house and 10 acres of land in Kennington itself, a small town on the outskirts of Invercargill.

We didn't integrate the businesses well. The manager at Kennington didn't co-operate properly with our staff, even though we traded everything as Southern Transport. In a similar situation today I would do things differently.

Another opportunity came by in April 1965. I was about to get married and had just obtained an option on R Hazlett and Sons in Drysdale Road, Myross Bush. Hazletts had been in existence for 42 years and they wanted to sell to Southern Transport. Marriage or not, they gave us the option and said they would wait until I came home, a generosity they confirmed to our competitors, Bob McDowell, of Makarewa, and Tom King, of Rimu Transport, when they tried to move in.

I had met Shona McKerchar at an ex-girlfriend's 21st birthday party. Born in Invercargill, Shona was raised on a family farm at Browns and educated initially at Winton and then for a couple of years at Southland Girls' High School. We were married in the Winton Presbyterian Church and spent our honeymoon in Dunedin and Queenstown.

On our return we faced an intriguing possibility. Ian Guise, a pretty aggressive carrier in Invercargill, who had started as a one-man band in 1955 and built up a tidy, 10-truck fleet, approached us to see if we were interested in putting our fleets together. Small carriers still exist, even today, but a trend was becoming obvious. Some small carriers had too small a base to grow from. They had proliferated after the Second World War because of their proximity to dairy factories but times were changing and mergers often made good business sense. Together we approached the Hazletts with a view to putting all three operations together. But neither Ian nor I believed we would make good deputies. The merger therefore didn't proceed. Ian and I continued to be in opposition for many years, sometimes friendly, sometimes not. But we got on well until his death in 1998.

Our deal with Hazletts was successfully concluded and we added five trucks – four Internationals and a Thames Trader – to our fleet, along with five acres of land and a depot.

That deal stretched the company financially. In 1967, while still in a tight situation, I was approached by Jack Hogan, a carrier in Steel Road, Lorneville, who had been in partnership with a recently-deceased brother. With no family Jack wanted to sell out. I told him I had no money, even though he was seeking only $3300 for his four trucks, three Bedfords and a Commer. I suggested another potential buyer to him. But Jack said he would wait until we did have the money. He said we had kept our word when we were in opposition to him and he felt that others hadn't. We took over his business in 1968.

By that stage I was the proverbial happily-married family man. Our son, Harold, had been born in August 1966 and our daughter, Jocelyn, arrived in February 1968.

In terms of business, however, I also had larger dreams. In the mid-1960s Dad and I went to Auckland and we visited United Concrete. At that time it was equally owned by Stevensons and David Lloyd and Co and it ran a large fleet of International and White concrete trucks. I remember thinking it was a line of business I would like to be in. United Concrete was a tidily run company, a combination of the construction industry that my family was so heavily involved in, and transport that I had just taken up.

Just after we were married Shona asked me: "What do you really want to do?"

"I would really like to own a business a bit like Stevensons in Auckland," I replied.

Dreams can come true, but you have to encourage them.

* * *

The company's operations remained inter-linked. Just before the Hazlett purchase Dad decided to get out of owning bush mills. There was no money in them. He had already closed the Blackhorn Sawmill, carting the logs to our Mokoreta Mill instead. The 30-mile rail restriction which forced us to take our logs to the railhead at Tokanui continued to be such a thorn in his side that he decided he had to get it out of his life forever.

From his years as a young man in Wyndham my father knew of a wagon trail that ran off the newly-finished Mokoreta-Tahakopa Road. That trail ran down a steep track through the bush to the Waikawa Valley Road. Dad figured that if he could have the track made into a road the timber from the Blackhorn and Progress Valley mills could be carted to a timber yard in Wyndham, which was only 27 miles from Invercargill. The company could therefore bypass the Railways altogether and tell the eagle-eyed station master what to do with his trains.

At first the Southland County Council member for the district – probably quite correctly – saw little value in the road, arguing it didn't service enough people. Despite being critically short of money, Dad decided to build it himself. Our old Cletrac dozer was put to work and a narrow but quite usable road was formed. During its formation the southern districts county member changed and Tom Buckingham, the newly-elected member, was more sympathetic. He told Dad that if we formed the road he would talk the county into gravelling it.

From the day the county-gravelled road was opened we never put another stick of timber on the Tokanui railway. We carted the timber to Wyndham into our timber yard or, if no one was looking, straight into Invercargill.

But not just a new road was needed for the sawmilling operation. It needed to be rationalised and made more efficient. The closure of the Blackhorn Mill, with logs then being carried to the Mokoreta Sawmill 16 miles behind Wyndham, was just a first step. Next Dad decided to close the other two mills – Mokoreta and Progress Valley – and build a new mill at Kennington on the 10 acres that came with Kennington Transport.

This was an amazingly bold step for the simple reason that we had no money. But Dad was convinced it could be built on a shoestring. He went to sawmill and dairy factory sales and the like, buying anything he thought he needed. When Nestles closed its factory at Underwood he bought the switchboard and transmission cases for driving roll cases. Many people wondered what he was going to do with

The Kennington Sawmill and its Fuji band saw were bold steps and proved my father right. He believed it could be built on a shoestring.

all the junk he accumulated. They found out he was going to build a sawmill, and he opened it in 1966 debt-free. It featured a Fuji band saw head rig, the first such saw in Southland.

It proved to be a good move. Southern Transport carted logs from Progress Valley to the mill on two second-hand Bedford 4x4s, one petrol, one diesel.

This coincided with a growing demand for pinus radiata timber and Niagara Sawmilling Company successfully tendered for a block from the Forest Service at its Pebbly Hills plantation not far from Dacre. Native timber was becoming hard to sell for construction work and we had to get into radiata pine to meet what the market wanted. It was our first attempt at milling radiata and Southern Transport desperately needed some better log trucks. We settled on two International Loadstar F1800 V8 petrol-engined trucks, a huge leap forward from anything we had had before. They were $13,000 each, which seemed like a fortune at the time. Fortunately, they turned out to be very good trucks compared with what we were used to.

*   *   *

The next transport expansion was to come in 1971 when we were approached by both Bob McDowell, of Makarewa, and Tom King, of Rimu Transport. They were sick of the transport business and wanted out. It was demanding and it could be unprofitable. I suppose we were the obvious purchasers.

Added to our fleet were three Leylands and three Austins from McDowells and two Fords, two Bedfords, an Austin Mastiff and a Mercedes 1418 from Rimu Transport. The Mercedes turned out to be the most notable part of the purchases. At that stage we had a large fleet of petrol-driven Internationals and Commers, because of previous bad experiences with diesel-driven trucks, although we still had some of the latter.

Mercedes vehicles were much more expensive. We paid $10,560 for the 1418, which was a lot of money for a second-hand truck. Then a curious thing happened. On the day we took over the company, Bill White, manager of Mercedes agents Cable Price, telephoned to ask if we had bought Rimu and the 1418. I confirmed we had.

"You're not a Mercedes operator," he said, "so I'll buy it off you for $15,000 which is probably more than you paid for it."

"Well, actually it is more than I paid for it," I replied. But its driver, Charlie Jack, was coming to work for us, and it had done only 113,000 miles. Further, Charlie had kept a notebook detailing every cent spent on it and the truck was remarkably economical.

"I think I'll keep it," I told White, "and see how long it goes before it needs anything else spent on it. Maybe I've been buying the wrong trucks."

When Charlie started with us I told him if he could get 200,000 miles out of the Mercedes without an overhaul, I would buy him another one. He came to me in 1974 to say that 200,000 miles had been reached. I telephoned Cable Price and asked what they would give us for the 1418.

"What did we offer last time?"

"Fifteen thousand dollars," I replied.

"What's it done now?"

"Two hundred thousand miles."

"Well, we'll still give you the $15,000."

"If they're that good, I'd better buy another one and I'll keep this one."

In the end, we sold it at 300,000 miles for $14,000. It turned out to be a very good investment.

We had always been great purchasers of International trucks which, until 1967, we bought through Universal Farm Machines, an associated company of Gormack Wilkes Davidson, Invercargill. That year we wanted two tractor units to pull bottom dumps on an Invercargill City Council gravel contract we had won.

I contacted Ron Scherp, the International salesman, and ordered a six-wheeler and a two-axle, which were worth about $20,000 in total. To my surprise Ron called on me about 90 minutes later to say he was sorry but he couldn't sell me the trucks.

"Why not?" I asked.

"Well, the powers-that-be reckon that if you go broke you'll take us down with you and they won't sell them to you."

I called the manager, John Clouston: "What's the problem, John?"

"The board is frightened of our exposure to your company," he said. "We have the recourse on your hire purchase deals." That meant if we missed our payments to the hire purchase company, Universal Farm Machines had to make them up.

"We've never missed a hire purchase payment in our lives," I told him. "We might be a bit slow paying our monthly accounts but we have never missed a hire purchase payment ever."

"I know that," John Clouston replied, "but that's what they think and they won't let me sell you the trucks."

I was pondering this setback when I had another surprise. A Bedford salesman from Gormack Wilkes Davidson arrived saying he had heard we wanted a couple of trucks. He would sell them to me.

"What if I go broke?" I asked.

"The boss reckons if you go broke Gormacks is big enough to stand it whereas UFM isn't."

"You can tell your boss," I said, "that I don't know what sort of trucks I'll be buying but they won't be Bedfords."

Once he had gone, I telephoned International Harvester's sales manager in Christchurch. Bob Gordon was livid because he was trying to sell Internationals and his own dealer was trying to put Bedfords into our fleet.

"Have you got 10 percent deposit?" Gordon asked.

"That won't be a problem," I replied.

"You've got your two trucks. I'll get them down to you."

There was a final chapter to this farce. John Clouston telephoned to ask who was going to get the commission on the two trucks.

"You'd better ask them that," I said, "but I hope it's not you." I never found out but we got the trucks and International Harvester got their money.

We bought more International trucks after that, to the point where they were too good to us. We were buying trucks that weren't right for our purposes but we kept buying them because the company treated us so well. Had they been tougher we would have changed to more suitable trucks more quickly.

Carting logs from Progress Valley provided a good example. It was a hard cart, of about 55 miles. But the first five or six loaded miles took up half the trip time. We were using petrol-driven V8 Internationals to cart long logs, buying them on a hire purchase agreement of one-third down and paying the rest over three years, our normal deal. But we were lucky to get two years out of them without having to give their engines a major overhaul. We never seemed to have any time when we weren't either paying them off or fixing them.

In 1971, I said to my father: "I think it's time we bought some better trucks

Once the business started expanding, Southern Transport's fleet started to look really impressive, even in a wet yard in Otepuni Avenue, Invercargill.

The $35,000 Leyland Crusader cost what seemed like a fortune but proved a classic example of value for money.

which have a bit more power."

A friend, Murray Drake, was a salesman for Leyland which had a model called a Crusader. It had an 8V-71 Detroit diesel, which was a two-stroke developing 290 horsepower, with a 15-speed Road Ranger gearbox. They cost $35,000, which seemed a fortune. Eventually I convinced Dad the firm could afford it and hopefully save some money on repairs and maintenance.

The thoughts of my family became clear not long afterwards when I met Dad and Ken while walking home for tea one night.

"Have you ordered that new truck yet?" Dad asked.

"No, I haven't."

That prompted Ken: "Are you frightened there's a dearer one you've missed somewhere?"

Expensive it might have been but its performance turned out to be another giant leap forward. It was the first new truck we bought that travelled 200,000 miles without having anything done to the motor. And there lay an economics lesson.

The Mercedes 1418 reinforced that. Once I had decided to buy a second Mercedes we decided to bale out of our petrol-engine fleet as quickly as possible. The diesel engines were far more reliable and fuel efficient than the American petrol equivalents. To aid the process I bought second-hand Mercedes trucks and the difference to the company's operations was very great indeed.

In a short time I had learned a lot in the real world of experience.

5

IN THE LATE 1960s AND EARLY 1970s the $100 million Tiwai Point aluminium smelter was being constructed on the windswept sand dunes across the harbour from the Port of Bluff. It was the culmination of nearly a decade of negotiation between the Government, which was selling hydro-electric power from the giant underground Manapouri scheme it was building, and Comalco Ltd, an Australian company jointly owned by the mining giant, CRA and RTZ. The Tiwai Point smelter would also have two Japanese partners. There was a lot of work to be done and, naturally, dollar signs flashed before many eyes at the thought of all those contracts and all that money.

In conjunction with A G Hoffman Ltd, whose principal, Gordon Hoffman, was a local contractor, we formed a company called United Plant Hire. We had previously mounted a 20-ton NCK crane on to an International chassis we had modified in our workshop into an eight-wheeler. We put that into United plant Hire. But there was also an opening at Tiwai for some Hamilton cranes, which were seven-ton cranes built on International tractors by C W F Hamilton, of Christchurch. We bought three of these and a Coles hydraulic crane and sold our NCK. United Plant Hire operated successfully for the entire construction period of the original smelter.

But huge construction or development projects also make some people act foolishly. The construction of the Tiwai Road along a bare access road to Awarua Bay, across a causeway and on to the Tiwai peninsula to the smelter site and wharf, was an example of this. The road to the causeway was largely over swamp and Wilkins and Davies had won the contract to build it, the causeway and bridge for $1,247,430.61. All had to carry huge weights and construction wasn't easy.

Wilkins and Davies were looking for carriers to cart thousands of cubic metres of gravel from the Oreti River and they knew the carriers would be clamouring for the work. They had been around for many years and naturally looked for the cheapest possible price. In fact they had managed to screw all carriers to about 6d (5c) a yard mile, which is calculated by multiplying the number of yards carried by the number of miles carted. I refused to work at that rate because it was ridiculously cheap.

One day, while I was sitting in my office, the telephone rang. It was Mac Tulloch, a well-known Mataura transport operator. I sat up because Mac and I had an interesting relationship.

About 1954, when I was just a youngster, Mac had won the Invercargill City Council base course gravel contract. The contract was to cart gravel from the Oreti River to rebuild many streets in Invercargill which had been badly neglected by a foolishly frugal council. Mac didn't usually work in the gravel contracting business. He was basically a rural carrier and, when he won the city's gravel contract, many local contractors were upset, accusing him of working for nothing.

In fact all he was doing was being more efficient. He put on 8 cubic yard bottom dumps, which he called Gravelmasters, as well as some conventional trucks. I remember their coming into the city with "Another Tulloch Transport" written on the fronts, and "Gravelmaster" along the sides. They were quite impressive for the times. From the mid-1950s until 1967, when we took the contract from him, he had probably 12 to 14 trucks working in the city.

We had won that contract thanks to a company called Allied Concrete which owned a gravel plant at Oporo on the opposite bank of the Oreti River from which Tulloch worked. Mac had bought a farm on his side to secure his gravel supplies for the contract. He and Allied Concrete did not get on at all.

That animosity became so bad that Allied Concrete approached me in 1967 to see if we would bid for the Invercargill City gravel contract, which was coming up for re-tendering for a two-year period.

"It'll be hard to beat Tulloch," I said.

Allied Concrete was determined, however. They promised to supply gravel very cheaply because of the way they felt about Tulloch. They were, in fact, prepared almost to give the gravel away. I wasn't prepared to look a gift horse in the mouth and the net result was that we won the contract. Mac lost, but he made Allied Concrete pay.

The road into its gravel plant travelled up the west side of the river, and Tulloch's farm was on the east side. In former days there had been a huge bend in the river which, over time, it had cut through to become straight. Part of Allied's road therefore then lay on the east side of the old river line and was on Tulloch's land because the survey was taken off the river line. The fact that the river had straightened out didn't alter the fact that Mac owned some land that was on Allied's side of the river.

One day after we won the contract Mac telephoned me. "Every time you go in there you're crossing my land. I'm going to put a gate across there and if you tamper with that, I'll prosecute you."

"How are you going to put a gate across there without crossing someone's land?" I asked.

"My man will row across the river and put the gate up. So you will have to shift the road in."

That, of course, was not my problem. It was Allied Concrete's problem. I told him he was just browned off because we had beaten him to the contract.

"No, I'm not," he said, before hesitating and adding: "Well, yes, I am."

"Well," I said, "at least you're honest about it."

Mac never did put the gate up but Allied Concrete had to alter the road into their plant at quite some expense to overcome the problem. As it turned out the City Council ran short of money in the first year of our two-year contract. We approached them saying we had made hire purchase commitments based on what they said they wanted and we would have to alter them. We asked for the contract to be extended to four years which the council had to agree to because they had let us down on quantities. That further annoyed Mac Tulloch, of course, because he had to wait four years to try

Our first 12 yard bottom dump was pulled by this International F1800.

At work on the Tiwai Road. It paid to hold out for the right price.

to win it back. He never did, and we lost it the next time as well.

Mac and I therefore always had a healthy respect for each other. So when he contacted me that day I was eager to find out what he wanted.

Mac is a forthright man. Was I carting any gravel on the Tiwai Road? No. Why not? I told him I believed 6d a yard mile was not enough; it should be 9d (10c). He said he agreed.

"They want my gravel," Mac continued. "They're short of raw material and I've got tons of it out there, as you know. But I won't deal with them. I don't like these people. They come down from up north and try to screw us locals. I've told them I won't deal with them any more and if they want to negotiate about my gravel they ring you."

"Why me?" I queried.

"You're there and you know the story." He was prepared to sell the gravel, and specified a price that wasn't unreasonable. He also wanted to have two of his trucks involved at 9d a yard mile. He added: "If I can get that they can have the gravel, provided you get any cartage you want."

I replied I wouldn't mind a couple of trucks at 9d a yard mile.

"That's the deal then," said Mac. "If they hire two of yours and two of mine, they can have the gravel. I've told them to come and see you. I won't talk to them any more." Not long afterwards a representative from Wilkins and Davies came to my office. Mac had told him to deal with me, he said, so what was the deal. When I told him he refused to pay the 9d and walked out.

He returned about a fortnight later.

"Look, we really need that gravel of Tulloch's," he said.

I shrugged: "What are you going to do about it?"

We went through the deal again.

"Right," said the Wilkins and Davies man, "if I can get one more truck on at 6d a yard mile, I'll let you and Tulloch have two on each at 9d. I would have to average it out."

It sounded reasonable and I agreed. He then asked who he should go to for the extra truck and I suggested Alister Ross in Gore because he had an eight-wheel Foden truck and trailer unit and was known to work very competitively. I telephoned him immediately and Ross agreed to work for 6.5d. The deal was done.

It turned out even more advantageously for us. The cartage for the road wasn't easy. The gravel had to be carted down the Tiwai Road, which was very soft, to the beginning of the northern side of the causeway which led to a bridge over the main channel in Awarua Bay. Trucks were regularly stuck and some even capsized into the mud alongside the road. All this delay only added to the difficulties of both Wilkins and Davies and the independent contractors who were being paid only 6d a yard mile.

After about two weeks Stewart Clark, of Wilkins and Davies, telephoned.

"Have you only got two trucks?" he asked "Put some more trucks on the job."

"No," I said, "the deal was that we could put only two trucks on at 9d a yard mile and I'm not working for any less."

"Forget about that," he said. "Get some more trucks on here. We have to get this gravel carted."

I telephoned Mac and asked if he wanted to put on any more trucks. No, he said. That left it open for us to put on several more.

The contractors had tended to start at the far end and work back because they were building the causeway across Awarua Bay to Tiwai Point at the same time. The independent contractors who had leapt in at 6d a yard mile thought they saw a chance to make up some money by negotiating a special rate over the causeway.

One Saturday morning a leader of the independent contractors telephoned to tell me they were on strike. They were not prepared to go across the causeway unless they were paid a special rate. They were trying to hold the job to ransom.

"Well, my trucks had better not be on strike," I said.

"No, they're not, but everyone else is," the man replied.

The TD15 bulldozers were put to good use on our various land-developing projects.

"This is not my argument," I said. "You don't want me in on it. I am not part of your deal. You did your own deal and I did mine."

"No, we want your support," the independent contractor said. "You have the most trucks on."

I drove to the site to find about 25 trucks lined up on strike, including the two Tulloch trucks.

"Does Mac know you've stopped?" I asked the Tulloch drivers.

"No," they replied.

"Then you'd better get back working," I replied. "You're not part of this argument."

They returned to work as I went into a meeting with a representative from Wilkins and Davies and the man who had telephoned me. A lively conversation began.

"We need a better rate if we are going to cross the causeway and we need your support," the leader of the contractors told me.

"I'm sorry, I can't support you."

"Why not?"

"I'd rather not tell you that."

"You're the biggest operator on the job here and we need your support."

"I can't support you."

I looked at the man from Wilkins and Davies, who had a twinkle in his eye.

"You may as well tell him," he said.

"It's like this," I said. "I'm actually getting more now than what you're asking for as your new negotiated rate to go across the causeway. So I can't really support you."

The independent contractor hit the roof. In fact, he did more than that. He walked off the job in disgust and refused to carry another yard.

He had only himself to blame. He had negotiated quickly, at a cheap rate, and tried to cut others, except for some of his associates, out of the work. It's typical of what happens on such jobs. People rush in and tend to work for nothing.

* * *

By the mid-1970s the Richardson family round-table discussions on the business covered many issues. Not only were we heavily into building and construction and transport we were also involved with land development and farming.

At Progress Valley Dad had bought 886 acres of worked-over native bush further along our original logging road to a place called Dummies Beach. With two TD15 dozers we cleared the bush, over-sowed the land and starting running sheep

Hard work and capital had by the mid-1970s turned our farms into desirable properties.

and cattle. Running the dozers and clearing the land at Progress Valley was a very expensive exercise, so costly in fact that we wouldn't do it today.

Between Waimahaka and Fortrose we bought a property called Rocklands Farm, and the next door neighbour as well, ending up with 775 acres. The land was over-run with gorse and the homestead was old and riddled with borer. There was only one decent shed and that was the implement shed. So we set to, building a new woolshed and homestead, fencing the property and spraying the gorse, some of which was subsidised by the Government.

For a longer term project, starting from 1973/74, we also bought 600 acres in the Hokonui hills and began clearing the worked-over native bush there and planting it in radiata pine.

All this was happening at one time, so we were extremely busy. We still weren't exactly rolling in money, but we were managing to pay our accounts better than we had in the past. We weren't helped by the oil price shocks of the early 70s, which affected all operators. We had too many petrol trucks and the massive price rises spurred us to speed up our diesel conversion programme.

But one of the developments that helped us with our finances had coincided with these projects. We had investigated buying Thomas and Co, a small sawmilling company in Mataura, which had a reasonable-sized forest nearing maturity. Our built-on-a-shoestring mill at Kennington was debt-free and we were able to borrow quite a lot of money against it in readiness for buying Thomas and Co.

Then we missed out. Graham McKenzie, one of its own shareholders, took it over. So we had this cash and suddenly we could get up to date with our accounts, something we probably should have done earlier. Richardsons were therefore on a much better financial footing. It made it much easier to trade and we had a better reputation with our suppliers. Above all we had money to buy equipment.

Graham McKenzie intended to export the logs the company owned. The price for export logs was reasonably high, higher than for domestic logs. But we couldn't buy Thomas and Co and outbid McKenzie with exports in mind because the Forest Service, our main supplier for radiata logs from the Pebbly Hills Forest, had made it very clear they would not sell logs at domestic prices to sawmillers who had their own logs and exported them. We needed the Forest Service and its logs for our sawmill. Graham McKenzie didn't have that concern. He was quite happy to take the gamble that exporting the logs would mean his own sawmill ran out of logs. His was only a small sawmill and, if it ran out of logs, so be it.

So we kicked up a fair old shindig when we discovered the Forest Service had decided they would give logs to McKenzie after all. Les Croswell, manager of the Kilkelly timber mill, and I flew to Wellington to meet Venn Young, who was then Minister of Forests, and told him what we thought of Forest Service policies. The Minister obviously listened to what we had to say because they reverted to the old policy which helped us to end up owning Thomas and Co after McKenzie had exported most of the forest.

Graham McKenzie also got us into another line of business. It was a boom time and he couldn't buy log trailers from recognised manufacturers. So he asked us if we would build him three, working out of the engineering shop we had for our own maintenance engineering. Those three successfully constructed, somebody else asked us to build a trailer and, before we knew where we were, we had a team of 10 or more engineers in our road transport engineering business building trailers, fitting bodies and hoists to new trucks and generally doing something we didn't originally intend getting into. We ended up making 49 heavy trailers and fitting dozens of hoists and bodies on to new trucks.

Farmers were also having a good time and buying lots of trucks. Our reputation spread. We did a lot of work and made many pieces of equipment. The only thing we didn't make was money. It was again a good lesson in not getting diverted into what you know only a little about. Engineering, in my opinion, is a highly specialist caper. Engineering companies therefore need to be specialised and employ people who have great attention to detail.

The engineering manufacturing business lasted a year or two. At the same time our land development projects at Progress Valley and at Hokonui were costing us a lot of money. We wore out dozers with monotonous regularity. We had been buying International TD 15 B and C dozers but better progress was made with a Caterpillar D6D and a very good operator. We also did quite a lot of farm development work for other people. That line of business also ground to a halt when the inevitable rural downturn struck and it was no longer economic to clear land in that manner for farming.

Still, we weren't going too badly as a business by this time. We may have been diverted occasionally but we were also making good decisions. It was also still a hands-on business. The after-hours telephone numbers included my own.

The transport fleet was also operating much better. We had bought the new Mercedes to replace the old one from Rimu Transport for $25,000, and 1974 was also the year we bought our first Mack truck.

We started buying Mack trucks more or less by accident. We needed another logging truck. Initially the Leyland Crusader had fulfilled all our hopes but some trouble had developed in the back end which, interestingly enough, was the only part that Leyland built. The engine and gearbox were built by American manufacturers Detroit Diesel and Eaton Fuller. It was ironic that the bit Leyland built gave us the problem.

However, I still felt some loyalty to International Harvester because of the way they had looked after us and despite all the troubles we had had with their trucks. So I ordered a model not previously available which had the same motor as the Crusader. But, for all sorts of reasons, it was held up and when we saw it wasn't going to arrive by the time we needed it we were getting desperate. Quickly, I ordered a Kenworth with a Cummins motor from Dalhoff and King. Amazingly it failed to arrive as well.

The Mack franchise had started in New Zealand in 1972 through Motor Truck Distributors. I had met its principal, Ron Carpenter, and he tried to convince me his trucks were the ones we needed. Mack was the only heavy American truck manufacturer to make all the parts themselves, including the motor, transmission and rear axles. At that time there were only three Mack trucks in the South Island and I was nervous. It meant you had to go to the Mack man for

Our first Mack truck proved to be so good we bought more and more.

An NCK crane mounted on a chassis built by us in our workshop, on the first International F1800 sold in New Zealand and bought second-hand by us.

your parts whereas parts for other American trucks were freely available from other sources.

But in 1974 we needed a truck – smartly – and Mack could supply. It cost $42,000 and it was No 44 in our fleet, an R685RS. It proved to be an excellent truck so the following year we bought a second one. The next year we bought a third. They were still the only Mack trucks in Southland at that stage but they were the first of a long line of Mack trucks we were to buy. In the meantime we had bought many second-hand Macks, either through our own endeavours or other takeovers.

The better trucks also meant I had time to concentrate on where the company was going. Trying to get broken-down trucks and dozers back into useful work while keeping the business going on a day-to-day basis had been a nightmare I didn't want to repeat. There had been no time to think about the long-term future, whether we were doing what we should be doing or whether we could do better the things we were doing. Getting into decent trucks made my life easier and gave me more time to consider our future.

* * *

Our own credit control had obviously improved as well. Just before Christmas we received from a local character called Jim Swaney a note written on an account we had sent him. "If you will possess your writhing tormented soul in patience your account for the year will be settled in due course when my work for the year is finished and, God willing, that will be December 12, 1974 when you make up your account for final payment," wrote Jim. He added: "Your seething excitement at the expectation of receiving $4 or so is exceeded only by ANZ Bank, Invercargill. So do not climb the hanging tree but have a joyful Christmas and come out fighting in 1975. Best wishes." Jim later found national fame through being the oldest motorcyling participant at the annual Brass Monkey rallies at Queens Birthday weekends in freezing Central Otago, until his death a couple of years ago.

Keith Cameron, who worked in Southern's office for 18 years, had sent the reminder and we had a good laugh at the reply.

Our credit control was good, however, when compared with some of the people we worked with. Archie Heenan was a carrier at Woodlands, near Invercargill, for 40 years and was once New Zealand President of the Road Transport Alliance. One of the infamous stories told about him was that he fell asleep during the Transport Minister's speech at one of the national conferences. He was expected to reply despite not having taken in much at all. Archie got up and said the Minister's promises were like tram tickets – good for the day of issue only. He just about brought the house down.

We used Archie to carry wheat from driers at Underwood, just out of Invercargill, to the port of Bluff. Country carriers in those days used to live off the cartage of lambs to Southland's meat plants, which was paid for by the meat companies. Any other work was sort of extra on top.

Archie would send out his bills once a year and he balanced in March. Towards the end of March we received an invoice from him saying: "To carting wheat, Underwood to Bluff last June, please fill in amount." That was typical of Archie. He didn't know how much he'd carted, but he did know he'd been there.

Another carrier like that was Dick Stewart, of Isla Bank, who ran quite a good transport business. He was known to let several years go by without sending out bills to farmers for general work.

He too lived off lamb cartage and every Tuesday he used to cart cattle from the Lorneville saleyards to the abattoir near Invercargill. Dick had a Sunbeam Alpine sports car and every Tuesday he would arrive at Lorneville in this car, round up his cattle, get a few trucks and cart the cattle to the abattoir.

Eventually Dick sold out. The man who took over didn't want to do that task and we were asked if we would cart the cattle.

"What's the rate?" I asked.

"Two shillings and sixpence (25c) a head."

"Okay, we'll do it. Who pays?"

"The butchers."

So we started carting cattle. As we sent out bills regularly we sent one to the butchers. It caused a great hue and cry. They weren't going to pay. They suggested the abattoir should pay. We sent the bill there. No, they didn't pay either.

"Well, someone has to pay," I said.

It turned out that Dick had been doing this work for years and years and never charged anyone. He just liked doing it. Times are not like that any more.

6

IN 1975 I GOT TO THINKING ABOUT ALLIED CONCRETE, the company that had been so helpful to us when we won the Invercargill City Council base course gravel contract back in 1967 because they didn't like Mac Tulloch. It was time to resurrect a dream.

Our relationship with Allied had continued when they gave us a contract to excavate their gravel from the Oreti River with a drag line at Oporo and take it to their plant. That had come about after I noticed the Dodge truck they used to carry the aggregate from Oporo to Invercargill was looking worn out. Allied was a public company and that means you can go to the Companies Office and look at their annual accounts. Being curious I did that and found Allied weren't doing too well.

I thought to myself, they'll be looking at that old Dodge and know it's had it. Then they'll go and get a quote for a new one and just about die of shock at the price. New Zealand was in the middle of a mad inflationary spiral and prices were rising all the time. We had earlier asked if they would let us cart their aggregate to Invercargill but they weren't interested. It was time to approach them again.

"What about we give you a price to cart your aggregate," I suggested to their manager.

"You've come at a good time," he said. "The old Dodge is about worn out. We've just got a price for a new one and it really horrified us."

"Well, I'll do you a deal," I said. "I'll buy your Dodge and I'll take over the job."

So the deal was done.

We carried the aggregate for a year or two until, in 1975, I thought it wouldn't be a bad company to own. It wasn't very well run and it never made much money. It had a poor fleet of concrete trucks, mainly two-axle with three-metre bowls. So I approached an accountant who worked for us and asked him how I would go about buying a public company. He shook his head and said he had no idea. He couldn't help me. That's a bit hopeless, I thought, and went away.

But the idea nagged at me. A year later I went to our solicitor, Lynton Laing, who later became a district court judge, and asked him the same question.

"I haven't got a clue," he said. "But I know a guy who will." He swung around in his swivel chair, picked up the telephone and dialled a number.

"I have a client here who wants to take over a locally-based public company and he doesn't know how to do it and needs some advice," he told his friend after getting through the niceties. "Do you think you could help him?"

A three-way conversation developed.

"The company he wants to take over is Allied Concrete. Who's your client?"

Gee, I thought, he's on the case.

"How does he know it's Allied Concrete?" I asked Lynton.

"There are only three Invercargill-based public companies," the voice on the telephone replied. "One is Southland Frozen Meat and it won't be that. Another is

J E Watson, stock and station agents, and it's unlikely to be them. So it's probably Allied Concrete."

He was dead right, of course, and that's how I came to hire the services of the voice who turned out to be Keith Skinner, a Dunedin sharebroker. He visited Invercargill to give me some advice and he turned out to be very useful.

We initially approached Allied to see if we could buy just a small interest, say, 25 percent, a seat on the board and the ability to give the company the sort of sort-out we thought it needed. They mucked us about for three months before replying no, they weren't interested. And by the way, they said, our Articles are such that you can't take us over. This got my back up. We had made what we thought was a very amicable approach and they had responded in a very confrontational manner.

Still, Allied Concrete did have some very unusual Articles. They stated, amongst other things, that it didn't matter how many shares you owned your maximum number of votes was 5000. Consequently no shareholder had more than 5000 shares. Its capital was low – $207,187. Its shareholders were widely spread but mainly Cantabrians.

The company had an interesting history. After the Second World War, Dal Fea, of Winton, who now lives in Invercargill, started a business called Farmers' Concrete Products, making concrete posts, troughs and the other products that its name implied. Throughout the 1950s and 1960s, as Southland farm production grew and grew, there was a huge demand. Dal had a business in the main street of Winton, which continues to this day under different ownership. He also had others in Otautau, Edendale and Oamaru.

Dal Fea became well established in the concrete business. He was also a shareholder in Concrete Blocks Southland Ltd, which was later taken over by Vibrapac South Island Ltd, a Christchurch-based public company in the concrete block manufacturing business. He also had shares and was a director of Southland Concrete Products in Tweed Street, Invercargill, which we later bought. At one stage he had been a director of the Southland Cement Company.

Dal had a cousin called Bill and he sold him his Edendale operation. Bill expanded to Gore with his newly named Fea Concrete Industries producing readymix concrete. Readymix concrete was a developing industry which had come about largely because it was getting harder to find builders' labourers to mix concrete on site. Further, quality was more consistent, while the sheer convenience of having a concrete truck arrive with your requirements at the time specified became more and

Transit Mixed Concrete was a forerunner to Allied Concrete, the company which led us to bigger and greater things.

This was Allied's fleet colour when we bought the company.

more appreciated. Then Bill decided to expand readymix further into Invercargill.

Readymix concrete was already available there through a company started by Jack Dundas, who had bought a company called A L Kelly Ltd, terrazzo sink top manufacturers in Clyde Street. Jack made the readymix and it was delivered by Southland Sand and Gravel, initially in tip trucks. Then they bought a couple of mixer trucks mounted on GMCs. As time went by they became involved with Certified Concrete, equally owned by Fletcher Construction and Winstones, which had started business in Auckland and Wellington in 1938.

To challenge Certified Concrete Bill Fea formed a company called Transit Mixed Concrete Ltd, a subsidiary of Fea Concrete Industries. It was called Transit Mixed Concrete after one of the two types of readymix plants. One is called a dry batch plant and the other a wet batch. A dry plant batches the materials and puts them in the back of the truck. Water is added and, by revolving the bowl, the truck does the mixing. When the materials are poured into the bowl from a dry batch plant and water added the concrete is mixed on the way to the job, hence transit mixed and Transit Mixed Concrete Ltd. At a wet plant, all materials including water are mixed at the plant and the concrete is tipped into the truck ready mixed. All the truck does is agitate the concrete on the way to the job.

But Bill Fea was short of money and he approached Neville Vincent, Chairman of Directors of Vibrapac South Island Ltd, the concrete block manufacturers, which bought out the Concrete Blocks Southland Ltd plant at Lorneville. Vincent was a sharebroker and he formed it into a publicly listed company called Allied Concrete. He was from Christchurch, which is why most of the shareholders were Cantabrians.

When the Allied Concrete directors rebuffed us, we were not put off. We decided to try to get a big enough interest in the company to influence the way it was run. Through a few friends we managed to buy 4 percent of the shares and didn't disclose our interest because we didn't have to. We also learned that if we made a bid for less than 50 percent of the shares we didn't have to give any notice. But if we were to bid for more than 50 percent we had to give two weeks' notice because that would constitute a takeover bid. Therefore, as we already had 4 percent, we decided to make an offer for 45 percent, which would bring us up to 49 percent.

We still wanted to do the deal amicably, however, and made a last-ditch attempt to get the directors to change their minds on voting rights. They wouldn't even agree to meet us. Through sources we discovered when the next directors' meeting was to be held and Lynton Laing, Cliff Broad, our accountant at the time, Keith Skinner, Ken and I just fronted up.

"We're here, we want to talk to you," I said. They reluctantly let us in and we stated our case. "We would like you to change your minds."

They replied they wouldn't, but they would discuss it while we waited outside. In reality, that meant standing on the footpath.

"I'm pleased it's not raining," quipped Lynton Laing.

Eventually, they invited us to return and asked for a copy of our accounts. "Why?" I asked

They were not sure we had enough money to buy Allied.

"That's really our problem," I said.

Obviously they were trying to be difficult. The Chairman made it clear they were not about to change the voting rights, even though everyone in the room knew they were going to have to change them shortly anyway. The Stock Exchange had already decreed that publicly-listed companies with restrictive voting clauses in their Articles had to remove them by 1980 or lose their public listing.

"Well," I said, "we're making a bid for 45 percent of the company and it'll be sent to shareholders in the night's mail."

How much per share were we prepared to offer, they asked.

"You'll have to wait until you get your offer in the mail," I said.

Once announced, even the Allied board conceded our offer of October 1976 was attractive. The company's shares had been selling for about 80c per $1 share. We offered $1.60 which resulted in an immediate influx of shareholders wanting to sell. In just over a week, we had just over 55 percent. But our offer was conditional. Directors had to agree to amend the Articles to allow one vote per share.

That condition made things difficult for Allied directors. In a press statement they admitted the offer was well above the market value but they did not want to amend the Articles, even though they were going to be forced to do so in a few years. That allowed us to take the moral high ground, questioning whether directors were acting in the best interests of shareholders and the company as a whole. The reaction to our offer showed shareholders had no problem with amending the Articles on voting rights.

We sought another meeting with them.

"Are you going to alter these voting rights?" I asked.

"No, why should we?"

The Allied Concrete colour scheme of blue cabs, yellow bowls and red hubs came from a Matchbox toy I bought Harold.

It was time to call their bluff.

"Because if you don't alter the voting rights we'll have to write to the shareholders and say we can't proceed with the bid for that reason. We'll point out that you have to alter them anyway by 1980 or lose your listing and, in the meantime, your shareholders will have lost the opportunity of getting $1.60 per share."

That set them thinking. When we met again they had changed their stance completely. They would alter the voting right clause if we altered our bid from 45 percent to 100 percent so that anyone who wanted to sell could sell. I think they were hoping to run us out of money.

"Okay," I said. And in a remarkably short time we had bought the entire company for just over $330,000.

One of the Allied Concrete directors had accused us of being a front for Fletcher Construction Ltd which already had a half-interest in Certified Concrete. He claimed Fletchers was putting up the money for our bid. By coincidence we had the bulk of the money to buy Allied on deposit at a local institution of which he was a director. I told him later he should have known we had the money available.

Another director was adamant we couldn't afford to buy Allied.

"You really think we can't afford this?" I asked him.

"Yes," he said.

"That would be because we were nearly broke 20 years ago."

He thought for a moment before saying: "Yes, I suppose that's right."

"A lot can change in 20 years," I said.

He had to concede that was true. I think he got the message that he shouldn't live in the past.

Another of the directors was Ralph Edgar, who had been a very successful Ford dealer in Balfour. I once asked him how he got into the concrete business.

"It was quite easy," Ralph replied. "I sold them three Thames Trader trucks which they couldn't pay for so I ended up taking the money in shares." In short, he was in whether he wanted to be or not.

In his final gesture as chairman, Neville Vincent took Ken and me to lunch at

The business end of a readymix concrete truck is more practical than pretty although keeping vehicles as clean as possible is a passion of mine. This was an example of how not to keep them.

the Grand Hotel, Invercargill, along with the board. This gesture tickled my fancy because they charged it to Allied Concrete which by this stage we already owned. So we really paid for the lunch ourselves.

We were delighted with the result, however. For a good price we had a readymix plant in Invercargill, another in Gore, a gravel plant by the Oreti River and 14 trucks, including 8 concrete trucks. But not so delighted were the company's management.

They had a top-heavy structure and I used to say they ran it like General Motors, even though it was a very small company. The first 12 months were rough. We had little co-operation. At one stage, a deputation of four of the hierarchy told me they didn't like the way I operated. One of their concerns was that I didn't wear a tie to work. Another concern was that I spoke to the drivers when it really wasn't my place to know them at all. I could see we weren't going to get on well.

Yet I also knew that my approach was better than theirs. At an early stage of the takeover battle I had met Dougal Soper, secretary of the Southland Drivers' Union, on a flight north.

"I hear you're buying Allied Concrete," he said.

"I'm trying to," I replied, "but they're resisting a bit. I think we'll end up getting it though."

"Well, I hope you do," Dougal said. "We've had an awful lot of industrial trouble out there. There are only about 10 staff in Invercargill in total. I'm only involved with the drivers and there are just five of them. But there's always some argument about something and I'm sure it's not the drivers."

We never had any industrial trouble at all. On one of my disapproved-of talks with the drivers I found one who had been there 18 months and had never met the general manager who worked on the same site. When I mentioned this to the general manager he told me it wasn't his job to know the drivers, it was somebody else's.

If you run a company that way you get the trouble you deserve and we straightened out those attitudes pretty quickly. The management and staff who didn't like working for us left. The secretary took off after telling me I was just a boy playing with trucks and would go broke. But others began to understand our reasoning.

"We've had a pretty rough first 12 months," I said to one chap who hadn't liked the way we had done things. "If you're prepared to give it another go I'm prepared to do so too."

"Okay," he said, "let's see if we can get on a little better." He's still with us as I write this.

It also helped that we bought a few new trucks and changed the fleet colours to our present blue and yellow with red wheels. Long before we bought Allied Concrete I had gone to town one Friday night and bought my son, Harold, a Matchbox toy truck in those colours. I liked them so we adopted them. They had the immediate effect of lifting our profile.

The first new trucks were two British Dodge Perkins V8 six-wheelers, but we needed something a bit better and asked Motor Truck Distributors to bring in some suitable Macks. I contacted Ron Carpenter one night about 8pm and told him of our problems with the trucks. He replied he would see what he could do with a cheaper model. At 8.30 the following morning, he rang me back.

"This is the spec, this is what it will cost you, this is the tare weight," he said. "If you order two, I'll bring in five." Ron had to order from the factory in the US in packs of five. The "spec" Ron spoke of was details of the componentry.

"That's okay," I said, "I'll take two." In fact, Ron brought in two packs, and we took five trucks. They were reasonably expensive but, with their reliability and longevity, they were great performers and lasted well. We sold the last of them in 1999.

We also received a tremendous boost when the Tiwai Point aluminium smelter was expanded in 1980, and Allied Concrete won a large contract for readymix.

Buying Timaru Readymix was our first move outside Southland, and one of the most significant in the company's history.

But even before that we got to thinking that perhaps we could expand a bit in the readymix business, although obviously enough it would have to be outside Southland.

* * *

Mentally, I ran up the South Island. In Dunedin Palmers ran a strong readymix business. They were well-established and unlikely to want to sell. My mind went on to Timaru, and stopped. Winstones was a large Auckland company established in the 1860s and they had a plant in Timaru they had inherited as part of their comparatively recent takeover of Vibrapac South Island Ltd, the block manufacturers. It was the only readymix plant owned by Winstones in the South Island, although they were quite big in readymix in the North Island, both under their own name and as half-owners of Certified Concrete.

I telephoned Winstone's head office in Auckland in June 1978 and asked who was in charge of the South Island. I was transferred to the appropriate director called Noel Gedye. I came to the point quickly. Would Winstones be interested in disposing of their readymix business in Timaru? He was just as direct in his reply.

"Yes, make us an offer."

I telephoned Noel again a week later and offered $130,000 for what amounted to four trucks and the plant on a block of land at Washdyke on the outskirts of Timaru.

"No, that's not enough," he said. "We want $210,000, but we'll come down and talk to you."

That's interesting, I thought. They'll come all the way from Auckland to talk to me even though they've rejected my offer. So they must be quite keen to sell.

Noel duly arrived with the South Island manager for Winstones. We talked for some time in my office, each putting our respective points of view. They came down in asking price and we went up to $140,000. We raised our bid by $10,000 only because we figured they were very keen to sell, as proved to be the case. They offered to go away while we thought about it.

Ken was with me. "No," he said, "We'll think about it now." Ken and I went outside, chewed it over and agreed we should go with the deal immediately. We returned to my office, confirmed the price and shook hands all round.

Then the director said: "We own 26 percent of a company called GE Tregenza Ltd, who are transport and aggregate operators in Timaru. We got this interest because they supply the aggregate to our readymix business and if we sell that business we'll have no further interest in Tregenzas. Would you be interested in buying our share?"

The only other shareholder, holding 74 percent, was British Pavements, a publicly-listed roading company based in Christchurch.

"Surely they have first option," I said.

"Yes, they do," the director replied, "but in the event that they're not interested, would you be interested?"

I replied that we could be but he should see how he got on with British Pavements first.

The two Winstones representatives left on a Thursday afternoon. On the following Saturday morning Winstone's South Island manager rang me to say they had been in touch with British Pavements, whose board had met on the Friday night. At that meeting, the South Island manager said, the board had decided to buy the remaining share in Tregenza and the readymix plant as well.

"That's going to be difficult," I said, "seeing you sold it to us."

"No," he replied, "we had an obligation to offer it to them at any price that you offered us."

"You never told us that," I retorted. "That was not part of the deal and, as far as I'm concerned, we shook on the deal of buying the readymix plant on Thursday and you were to offer them your shares in Tregenza. That was a different deal altogether."

"Oh, no," he replied, "the people who own British Pavements are real gentlemen and we couldn't do that to them."

"Well," I fired back, "it's a pity you weren't the same."

The South Island manager was a bit upset about that remark and we terminated the conversation fairly tersely.

An hour later, Noel Gedye telephoned from Auckland.

"They tell me you're not very happy."

"No, I'm not."

"Well, I've gone over my notes and I can see that we may have misled you. We will honour our deal to sell you the readymix plant and will face the wrath of British Pavements."

"Fair enough," I said.

And the deal was done. British Pavements were extremely annoyed. Winstones had a director on the Tregenza board and he did not know it was for sale. Worse than that, two months before I approached them British Pavements had asked Winstones whether they would consider selling their readymix business to Tregenza and offered them $180,000 for it. Winstones turned it down flat, saying

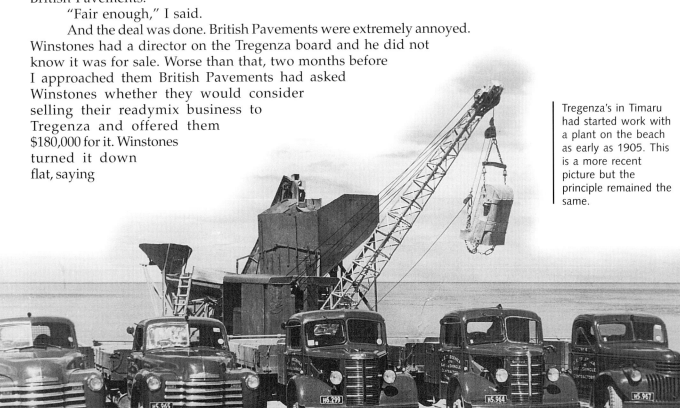

Tregenza's in Timaru had started work with a plant on the beach as early as 1905. This is a more recent picture but the principle remained the same.

it wasn't for sale. Then, just eight weeks later, we had bought it for $140,000. British Pavements had not been informed, or even the Winstone director. To cap it all off, the manager of Tregenza was about to recommend that his company go into the readymix business.

This isn't an ideal situation, I thought to myself. Tregenza was the only aggregate supplier in the area at the time. It was threatening to go into business against us and there was already one opposition company, Precision Concrete, in Timaru. You'd better go and meet the British Pavements people, I told myself.

In Christchurch, British Pavement's director, Clem Paterson, turned out to be truly a gentleman and one of the finest people I would ever do business with. He told me their side of the story and concluded: "We are naturally annoyed."

"I can understand that," I said.

"We were prepared to give them $180,000 for the business," he said. "We will give you that and it will be the fastest $40,000 you'll ever make."

"I don't really want to do that," I said. "That's not why we bought it."

Clem Paterson took that in and replied: "I'll give you my word that we won't go into the readymix business without talking to you again and, in the meantime, we'll continue to supply you with aggregate."

* * *

Looking back, that move into Timaru was one of the most significant in the company's history, a stepping stone that would lead eventually to expansion throughout the country. Comparatively speaking it may have been relatively small but it set in train further expansions and gave us an indication of what could be achieved. One day Timaru, the next day . . . who knows?

We called the company Timaru Readymix, but we had not been going long before Precision Concrete decided to sell out. Sixteen years previously the owners had sold to Vibrapac (later Winstones) the plant that we now owned and had then started up in opposition. That naturally had caused some bitterness and there had been a 16-year battle.

Precision Concrete offered itself to various companies, including British Pavements, Fulton Hogan and us. Clem Paterson telephoned me.

"What are we going to do about this, do you think?" he asked.

"I don't know," I said. "Maybe we should have a think about the whole situation."

"Well, Winstones wants to sell their 26 percent of Tregenza and, as far as we're concerned, we're not going to buy it? Do you want to buy it?"

"Yes, I suppose we could," I replied.

"Well, you have my absolute assurance that whatever you offer them we will not match. Under the pre-emptive rights they have to come back and offer the shares to us at whatever your offer is. We have the last right of refusal. So you can buy them for whatever you can get them for."

We therefore ended up doing a very good deal, buying 26 percent of Tregenza for $70,000, although we'd discovered the company wasn't making any money. Clem wasn't sure what was wrong. It actually lived off the 40 miles railway restriction then in force (expanded since our sawmilling days at Tokanui) because it had the only licence to cart building materials from Christchurch to Timaru. Under the old restriction the company had made a lot of money through this licence, running just one truck full-time against the Railways. It gave good service, far better than Railways, and charged profitable rates.

But when the restriction was extended to 150km carriers could just about sneak from Hornby on the southern extremities of Christchurch to Washdyke at Timaru's northern boundary. That made it harder to police and, although Tregenza was still doing well from the work, others were cutting away at it. Unfortunately, the rest of their operations were highly inefficient. Tregenzas had been a successful company that had lost its way.

The Tregenza fleet was well known in South Canterbury and it wasn't hard to make it more efficient.

E G Tregenza had started the business back in 1905, down on the Timaru foreshore, digging gravel from the sea. His son, G E Tregenza, had taken it over and formed it into a company with several local partners undertaking mainly gravel extraction and contracting work until, in 1965, he had sold to British Pavements, which controlled the company from that point. Later, Winstones had become involved.

My years in the transport industry had by then given me considerable experience in profitability and productivity. Some of that experience was basic. Trucks and other equipment made money only when they were working. It made economic sense to have trucks loaded both ways and you had to have the right type of equipment for the job at hand. As a part-owner I wanted to become involved in Tregenzas.

My initial inquiries showed that, apart from a motor scraper, grader, a few loaders and similar gear, it had 14 drivers, 27 trucks, five mechanics and seven in the office.

"No wonder it's not making any money," I said to Clem. "For every driver we have two trucks, for every three drivers, roughly, we have one mechanic and for every two drivers we have one in the office."

More than that, some trucks were worn out and new trucks had been badly chosen. I liked to talk to drivers because they often had shrewd ideas about the transport industry and the company they worked for.

"Can I come for a ride with you?" I asked a Tregenza driver one day. His truck, an articulated Commer with an eight-yard tipper, was as neat as a pin. He agreed and, as we drove off down the road, he turned to me.

"This is a turn-up for the books," he said.

"Why's that?" I asked.

"I've been driving here for 23 years and this is the first time I've seen a boss inside a truck."

"Is that right?" I responded, not really surprised. "Tell me, this truck has a petrol engine?"

"It's got a V8 Chrysler petrol engine," he replied.

"It would be a bit under-powered, wouldn't it."

"Under-powered!" he exploded. "We were carting tallow from Pareora, which is just south of Timaru, to Christchurch, and I had 10 tons on this truck. One of those big Fusos [Tregenza did have a couple of decent 300 horsepower Fuso diesels] had

20 tons, and we both headed off to Christchurch in a howling north-wester.

"I was still going up and met the Fuso coming back just north of Ashburton. That's how much use this thing is. And if you take that book out of the glove box, you'll see how much time we spend off the road with the trucks I drive." He drove two different Commers and the down-time was mind-boggling.

On another day I was at Tregenzas for a meeting. I had taken Harold, who was just 13, and sent him away on a truck for a ride while I attended the meeting. We were driving home after the meeting, when Harold asked me if I had seen a large heap of sand on a beach at Normanby. I replied that I hadn't.

"Well, you want to go and have a look," he offered. "There's a whole heap of trucks down there and they're loading them with an old Fordson loader that has a bucket that you have to hit on the ground to get it to return." I knew Harold was referring to a mechanical trip bucket and if he could see obvious inefficiencies why couldn't somebody else.

At the first available opportunity I asked the foreman: "How come you're loading that fleet of trucks with that old Fordson with a mechanical trip bucket when you have two decent loaders sitting here in the yard not working?"

"We're not allowed to use those because the powers-that-be reckon there's no money using big loaders to load our own trucks. We keep them there in case someone rings up and wants to hire them."

Fleet utilisation was just as shocking. One month the freight truck with the restrictive licence on the Christchurch run earned more money than all the other trucks in the fleet put together. Fleet purchasing was unbelievable, based mainly on price. On one occasion I walked past two new Commers.

"Are these Commers identical models?" I asked the head mechanic.

"Yes," he said.

"How come one is on eight-stud wheels and one is on 10-stud wheels?"

"Oh, you noticed that," he replied.

"Naturally."

"Well, the one on 10-stud wheels is an artic and when we got it new and put it on to that artic, we thought the rear axle was too light to pull it. So we took the rear axle out of the truck that this one was replacing, which was a heavier model, and put it under there. When we did that we discovered that because it was a heavier model it had 10-stud wheels. This one then had 10-stud wheels on the rear and 8-stud on the front. So we took the front axle out of the old one and put it under the new one to get them even. That's why this one has 10-stud wheels and the other one is an 8-stud."

"So you have a brand new truck with the axles out of its predecessor under it and a V8 engine pulling it. It hasn't got a lot going for it, has it?"

"No," the mechanic agreed, "not really."

But what were we to do about Precision Concrete. They wanted $140,000 for it. We had paid the same amount for the Winstone's plant and $70,000 for the 26 percent share of Tregenza. I suggested to Clem Paterson that Richardsons buy another quarter-share in Tregenza and British Pavements buy Precision Concrete for $140,000. We could then put into Tregenza our respective readymix plants because they were equal in value.

"Then we'll be even," I said.

"Okay," Clem agreed.

"What do you want for your quarter-share in Tregenza?"

"Well, it hasn't made any money since you bought Winstone's quarter-share, so I don't suppose it's worth any more."

That, I thought, was generous because British Pavements had helped us screw Winstones down. So, for another $70,000, we bought another quarter-share of Tregenzas, which took us to equal ownership with British Pavements. In the end, however, we discovered that Tregenzas bought the other plant, not British Pavements, so we had put in an extra $140,000 which had to be paid back to make us even. It was an unusual way to get into the business.

Clem and I were discussing all this in a room in the Grosvenor Hotel, Timaru, one night.

"Do you want to be chairman?" Clem asked.

"I don't care. Hang on a minute." I took a 20c coin from my pocket and asked Clem to call. He won, and was chairman of Tregenzas under the new structure. But we also had sufficient clout to sort the company out. We bought some new trucks, while cutting down Tregenza's fleet considerably.

The company had an unusual system with its articulated trucks. It had one type of turntable for the tipulators and a different kind of turntable for the flat decks. There were 10 artics in the fleet for the five drivers, because drivers used one tractor unit if they were pulling a tipping trailer and another if they were pulling flat decks.

Mum and Dad. His death in 1979 was extremely sad because he was only 63.

"Why don't you standardise the turntables?" I asked one day.

"You can't pull tipulators with quick-release turntables," somebody replied.

"We have a fleet of tipulators with quick-release turntables in Invercargill, and I don't see why Timaru is any different," I replied. We standardised the turntables and sold five tractor units immediately.

About this time, Clem invited me to join the board of British Pavements, which had similar problems with its fleet. Perhaps I had a reputation as a trouble-shooter for I was asked to help sort out that company's fleet as well.

When we went into 50-50 ownership of Tregenza we insisted on a clause in the Articles. British Pavements, which was to change its name to Pavroc Holdings after a merger with a private company, was a publicly-listed company and our clause stated that if Pavroc Holdings as it was then known became the victim of a successful takeover, Richardsons had the right to buy the other half of Tregenzas.

Our insistence on this clause had aroused some questions. I pointed out the company might get taken over by a company we did not want to be in partnership with.

"Fair enough," said Clem "We'll agree to that if you agree to have a clause in the Articles that reads the same as far as we're concerned."

"That doesn't worry us at all," I replied. "We know whether we're going to be taken over or not whereas in a public company you never do."

A lot had been happening in a short time and it paid to be cautious.

* * *

In February 1979, my father died. He and Mum had shifted to a 42-acre farmlet in 1974 and that allowed Shona and me to shift back to the family home in Inglewood Road, where we have remained ever since.

After suffering his brain haemorrhage Dad had taken an active part in the business for about 10 years. Then, from the early 1970s, he started to suffer a series of strokes. From that time on his main interests were in the farms and the land-clearing operations although he was still involved in the decision-making for the overall company. During this time Ken looked after the building company and I looked after farming, land clearing and forestry operations as well as the transport and concrete companies.

Dad's death was sad. After his brain haemorrhage we were told he would be old before his time. When he died he looked about 80. He was, however, just 63. His huge influence on my life and my way of thinking would remain.

7

TIME MOVES QUICKLY IN BUSINESS. A close neighbour to Southern Transport was Otepuni Transport and, in 1979, we bought the bulk side of that business. In physical terms that was just a couple of trucks but it gave us some additional places on the roster for carting phosphate from the port of Bluff to the phosphate works at Awarua, which over the years was to become a large part of our business.

The following year we bought Purdue Bros, one of Southland's better known transport firms, and it was unique. Syd Purdue had started the business in 1946 and older brother George had joined about a year later. In all that time it had never been in overdraft and always had cash in the bank or, as Syd used to say, "in the tin." George was the boss but Syd had a large part to play in the business as well. I had a lot to do with Syd, who had a great sense of humour.

One day I was at their office when a driver behind the wheel of an old Bedford arrived and parked the vehicle outside the front door.

"Are you finished that job?" Syd roared at him.

"No, I'm not," the driver said. "The petrol is pouring out of a big hole in the bottom of the tank."

"Well, you keep pouring it in the big hole at the top and don't come back until you've finished," Syd yelled back.

On another occasion while I was there, Syd sent a driver away in a flat deck Bedford with a hoist. It had no sides and the hoist was used for unloading timber and the likes. But Syd wanted the driver to use the truck to cart some concrete gravel.

"Get three yards and put it on the truck," he ordered. "Then deliver it to the job."

"There are no sides on the truck," the driver objected.

"Be careful when you put it on," Syd said. "Taper it up and drive carefully."

"There's no shovel on the truck," the driver objected further.

"You don't need a shovel," Syd said. "Just carry on."

The driver left. A short time later, he called up on the radio telephone. He had reached the job, and his vehicle was stuck.

"Well, scoop the mud out from under the wheels and shovel some gravel in there," Syd advised. "You'll soon be out."

Purdue Bros trucks were familiar sights on Invercargill streets.

George and Syd Purdue in 1966. We bought the well-known Invercargill carrying company in 1980 and, as the picture indicates, they were a couple of characters.

The driver replied patiently: "What with, my bloody fingernails?"

Syd looked at me and said: "There's no answer to that, is there?"

Purdues had a Drott front-end loader, an International-based crawler mounted loader. The driver would drive the loader up ramps and on to the truck deck then drive himself to the next job. Then the driver lost his licence through a traffic offence. He could drive the Drott on the job but he couldn't drive himself to the next one.

Syd got around this problem by getting the driver to contact the office when he had finished. Syd would then bike to the job, throw the bike on the back with the loader, drive to the next job, then bike back to the office.

I was there once when Syd arrived back at the office puffing heavily.

"There's no bloody justice in the world," he complained. "He loses his licence and I end up riding the bike."

That was the way they operated, but while they were rough and ready in some ways they ran a very good business. About eight years earlier Purdues had bought another carrier, Bill Valli, who had run trucks for many years, and they had also bought out Tommy Martin, a one-truck operator with an immaculate 1934/35 Chevrolet, who for a long time did all the cartage for Georgeson's Joinery.

They also had a Morris Commercial with a Saurer diesel engine. Saurer was a Swiss motor, made under licence by Morris, and had a poor reputation. Once, I asked Syd how the Saurer was performing.

"The longer we own it the sorer I get," he replied.

George's son, John, stayed on as a one-third shareholder to run the business after we took it over. Syd's philosophy of having money "in the tin" had worked reasonably in days of low inflation but high inflation meant they never had quite enough to buy new trucks.

Within a few short years, borrowing against the company's assets, we had spent $1 million re-equipping Purdue Bros. Apart from the shares we had bought

Part of the Purdue Bros fleet at the time we bought the company.

we had
invested no further money
in the company, and neither had John.
It was simply a case of making the company's money
work for us. Having it "in the tin" wasn't good enough.

* * *

In December 1980, Fulton Hogan Holdings Ltd, the Dunedin-based road contracting company, made a takeover bid for Pavroc Holdings. The battle began a couple of days before Christmas. John Fulton, Fulton's Managing Director, with whom we had a very good relationship, contacted me to advise me of the development.

This is going to be interesting, I thought. Pavroc Holdings was still controlled by the founding family of British Pavements. In the event, it was no fait accompli because there was some quite spirited opposition. Some of the Paterson family, the major shareholders, wanted to sell. But other shareholders didn't want to sell, so it was all a bit messy.

Clem Paterson had hired a new manager for Tregenzas and had promised him shares in the company. That was difficult to satisfy because, in a 50/50 company, if both shareholders sell some shares, the third party, who might hold only 10 or 20 percent of the shares, holds the balance of power.

The battle for Pavroc was taking some time so I approached Fulton Hogan to exercise our pre-emptive rights over Tregenza and they agreed. Once that was successfully completed, we sold a third share to the manager.

The takeover for Pavroc was fought mainly by one shareholder and one family member and, in the finish, Clem's brother, Graham, and a man called Martin Coffey, won out. Coffey owned 25 percent of Pavroc and Graham Paterson 10 percent. They decided they would not sell to Fulton Hogan.

All of this coincided with our advance into Christchurch, the South Island's largest city. That move came about through unusual circumstances. In 1980, when our reputation in readymix was obviously growing, two individuals approached us to go into business in that city with another contractor. Originally they wanted us to back them into a readymix business and I was reasonably interested. But one of them then approached an aggregate company and its principals wanted to join in as well. This, of course, was relayed back to me.

"I've never dealt with them and I don't know them," I said. The contractor's representative came to Invercargill and checked us out in a rather superior manner, after which they said they thought we were all right and I said I was pretty relaxed about them. The deal was struck with our holding 30 percent, the contracting company holding the same percentage and the two individuals holding 25 and 15 percent respectively.

The business was an immediate success but I would have to say they were the most unsatisfactory partners I have ever had the misfortune to be in business with. They used us to get any information or buying privileges possible. Any experience we had they took and, when they had it, they wanted us out.

The reason they gave for wanting to get rid of us was that I had bought a shareholding in Farrier Waimak, another concrete company, which had come about through fortuitous circumstances. When the others in the initial Christchurch business showed concern I offered to sell my shares but the initiator of that venture said he didn't want us to sell, so we didn't. Later he changed his mind and used, to my way of thinking, an unethical method to get us out.

Their ways were well illustrated at one board meeting and showed all too clearly what we were up against. The contractor's board representative gave the impression that he thought his Southland partner was somewhat inferior to him. He arrogantly turned to me and said he had had my 30 percent of the company valued. It was worth, according to this valuation, $180,000. He would give us $200,000 for our shares.

"And any man who turns down $200,000 for 30 percent of this company is a fool," he said.

"Is that right?" I said. "Well, I'll tell you what. I'll give you $400,000 for your 30 percent in the company."

This was no idle bluff. I had the money.

"I'll have to think about that," the contractor said.

Based on what he had just told me that shouldn't take long, I told him.

He returned to me later, saying he would not take up my offer. Then he asked me: "What are you going to do?"

"I'll wait," I said.

"What do you mean?"

"Well, put it this way. I'm 45 and you're 72."

When he died I sold the shares to his widow for $200,000.

Our Farrier Waimak involvement began through Martin Coffey, who not only owned 25 percent of Pavroc Holdings but also 40 percent of Farrier Waimak, which was involved in aggregate production, road sealing and construction and readymix concrete. Established in 1919, Farrier Waimak had been listed publicly for about 30 years. It had begun as Farrier and Walker partnered by Harry Farrier, an Australian immigrant who started with £500 his wife had had left to her by her father, and Tom Walker. That partnership lasted until 1932, shortly before Tom's death.

Then it became Farrier and Co. At different times subsidiaries were formed, two of which were Waimak Shingle and Sand, which did as its name implied from the Waimakariri River near Christchurch, and F J Perham Ltd, a carrying company. Later, Road Pavers Ltd, which tar-sealed roads, was established. In 1955 it was floated as a public company called Farrier Waimak and at its peak it had about 200 staff as it expanded into concrete block production in 1967 and readymix concrete the year after, operating out of Coutts Island where the gravel plant was. At the end of 1972 they took over Associated Concrete in McAlpine Street, which is where our plant is today. When we became involved they had 17 percent of the bitumen market and a reasonable share of the concrete business in the area.

Martin Coffey, who ran a business called Coffey's Accommodation Bureau at the top end of Colombo Street, Christchurch, quietly bought shares in publicly

Early days at Farrier Walker, which was established in 1919.

In 1932, Farrier Walker became Farrier and Company Ltd. This photo was taken in 1944 and shows their longstanding preference for International trucks.

listed companies. His ambition was to amalgamate Pavroc Holdings and Farrier Waimak and he was, in fact, dead right in his thinking. One had a large roading business and aggregate plants while the other had reasonable aggregate plants, a small roading business and readymix concrete. Readymix concrete takes the balance of production from an aggregate plant. Material that isn't used in making roading chip can be made into concrete aggregate. Pavroc Holdings didn't have that outlet for its undersized stone so it would have been an ideal marriage.

But Coffey couldn't get the respective boards to agree to this and he kept buying shares in both companies until he was close to the point of holding considerable sway and therefore a lot closer to achieving his goal. But his plans were thwarted when Fulton Hogan came along and made its takeover bid for Pavroc. That was one reason why he did not wish to sell his shares. The second reason was that he didn't think Fulton Hogan was offering enough.

I didn't know Martin Coffey but I knew his background and I went to visit him one day, having long believed in the direct approach.

"What are you going to do with your 40 percent shareholding in Farrier Waimak?" I asked.

"I'm not sure. Do you want to buy it?"

"Yes, I'd be interested."

"Who owns your company?"

"My brother and I."

"A private company?"

"Yes."

I will always remember his response.

"I'll sell my shares to you. I don't like these public companies where the directors play golf in the shareholders' time."

We did a deal for an agreed price and he asked me to come back in a week. I returned to find him in his office with his share certificates scattered all about. He had with him a foolscap pad and a ballpoint pen. He scribbled out the basis of the deal before handing it to me saying: "Sign that."

I handed him a cheque of about $480,000 for nearly all of his shares because he wasn't sure how many he had. We agreed I would pay for any more later and we both signed the piece of paper which constituted our agreement.

"I wouldn't mind a copy of that," I said, so we drove to the nearby Edgeware Village where Martin handed over 15c to put the piece of foolscap paper through a photocopying machine, and I flew home to Invercargill.

It was time to move again. I telephoned our local sharebroker the next day.

"Put a buy out on the market for 10 percent of Farrier Waimak, please," I asked.

"What are you going to do with 10 percent?" he asked.

"You'd be surprised. Just put the buy out, please."

"Ten percent isn't much good," he persisted.

"It'll be okay in this instance," I said.

The following morning, John Fulton telephoned me.

"Someone's put a buy out for 10 percent of Farrier Waimak," he said. "I wonder who that is."

"I wonder," I deadpanned.

"I think it's you."

"What makes you think that?"

"Well, the bid comes from Invercargill. Who else would it be?"

"I guess that's fair enough. It is us."

"Well, I hope you have more luck with Martin Coffey than I've ever had."

"I think so. I did it differently."

John Fulton was puzzled. "What do you mean by that?" he asked.

"You went to see him last, I went to see him first."

Fulton twigged. "You've already got his 40 percent."

"That's right," I said.

"And that's why you want 10 percent."

"Ten percent will do in the meantime."

We managed the 10 percent and control of Farrier Waimak immediately. It was a struggling company, not making any money. Its principals didn't like spending capital on plant so it was quite run down. Staff numbers had been reduced to 73. But it was basically sound. All it needed was somebody enthusiastic enough to spend some money wisely and get its gear up to date. Its other major shareholder was Golden Bay Cement Company, which owned 24.9 percent, and a deal was soon done to buy that holding as well.

As this was happening I met a man called Avon Carpenter who was, amongst other things, chairman of directors of a privately owned company called Roberts Concrete in Mount Maunganui and Tauranga. In passing conversation he asked me if I was going to use Farrier Waimak as a vehicle to float the rest of the Richardson enterprise as a public company.

"Definitely not," I said. "We'll be going private, not public."

"Oh, I thought you might go public," he said. "You're big enough."

"We're probably big enough," I conceded. "But I don't want to. I'm not interested."

Farrier Waimak's concrete trucks were painted traditional Canterbury colours.

About a week later, Carpenter telephoned me in Invercargill, and asked if I were serious about going private with Farrier Waimak. I replied I was.

"Well, I want a public company and I'll do a deal with you," he said.

If we sold him the 76 percent of Farrier Waimak that we owned he would sell us all the physical assets back.

"We'll change the name and you can form a new company called Farrier Waimak 1984 Ltd and carry on in business doing what you're doing, and I'll have the 76 percent of a cashed-up public company which I want to do other things with," Carpenter said.

We agreed to put the proposal to the remaining shareholders, who agreed and the deal was done. We sold our shares at what I thought was a very good price, and bought back the assets of what amounted to 100 percent of the company for $1.4 million.

This exercise taught me a lot about the sharemarket. When Farrier Waimak owned the original business, the $1 shares were selling on the sharemarket for about 80c. We paid $1.4 million for the assets and, as soon as we did this, the company's share price jumped to $5. There were 600,000 shares in the company so market capitalisation at that price was $3 million. But the company's only asset was $1.4 million of cash. I could understand a company being under-valued or over-valued when it owned physical assets but I found it difficult to understand how $1.4 million worth of cash was suddenly worth $3 million.

When I asked this question aloud, I was told: "You just don't understand the sharemarket." I didn't then, and I don't now.

I also did a deal to sell to Fulton Hogan, which had finally managed to buy Pavroc, the road construction and sealing division in November 1983. We kept the readymix concrete division at Sockburn and shingle yards at Coutts Island, Belfast, and Pound Road, Yaldhurst, and continued rationalising the entire operation to make it more efficient. Four years later we sold the aggregate division to Fulton Hogan as well, leaving us just the readymix concrete business, which was what we wanted in the first place. Selling off the other operations provided us with the capital to improve equipment and plant.

* * *

On one occasion we expanded when I didn't want to, but it turned out well anyway. We had bought into Tregenzas in 1980 and two years later bought Francis Construction Services bin services and some other operations they ran. The other bin operator in Timaru was Freightways, a publicly-listed company operating throughout New Zealand. Freightways was not really in the rubbish business but in Timaru they had one truck and 45 bins. That would fit in nicely with our business, I thought.

For 18 months I tried to buy Freightways bin service but the company was only interested in selling the entire operation. I was reluctant because Freightways was a town carrier and I didn't want to be in that segment of the market. Further, the whole operation consisted of only eight trucks, four trailers and a forklift. All their land and buildings were leased. I kept telephoning Freightways to buy part of their business and they kept telling me to "buy the whole lot."

Finally, their New Zealand manager telephoned and asked if I would be in Christchurch shortly. I said I would be and we agreed to have breakfast at the Russley Hotel.

"By the time you've had your breakfast, you'll own Freightways Timaru," he said.

"There is no way I'm going to buy Freightways Timaru but I will meet you for breakfast," I said.

He was right. By the time breakfast was over, I had bought Freightways Timaru. They wanted $130,000 initially, and I bought it for $67,000. The deal was done.

Right: The only new concrete truck ever purchased by Farriers until our takeover, an International ACCO 1930A, taken at the Coutts Island gravel plant.

We carted bridge beams into difficult spots.

On the way back to Invercargill I called in at Tregenzas and told the staff we had bought Freightways.

"What do we want that outfit for?" was the first question.

"Well, we wanted the bin business and now we have the whole lot," I replied.

I arrived back in Invercargill and the next morning I was contacted by a Timaru carrier, Ian Frew, who ran a tidy carrying operation from Washdyke, on the outskirts of the city.

"Gee, you've got to get up early in the morning to beat you," he said.

"How's that?" I asked.

"I've been trying to buy Freightways Timaru for two years," he said.

"Well," I replied, "I've been trying not to buy it for 18 months. We must have been dealing with a different person." It turned out we had been.

I explained I really wanted only the bins and he asked if we would sell the rest to him. I said we would.

"I'll give you what you paid for it," Ian said.

"No, you won't," I replied. "You make me an offer."

He came back with an offer that was considerably more than we had paid.

"That sounds okay," I said, and we did the deal. We owned the company for about a month.

Some time later Ian said to me: "I probably paid you more than you paid for the business."

"You did actually," I replied, "but you were happy."

"I was delighted," he agreed.

"I was delighted as well," I said. "So everyone's a winner."

Eventually we bought Francis Construction's depot and took over its rock cartage contract as well.

* * *

There was much to keep us busy. In 1983 we also entered into an equal partnership with Fulton Hogan to buy 50 percent of Daveys Concrete Ltd, of Balclutha, a small readymix business but a larger operator in pre-cast, pre-stressed concrete. The business was in the midst of a building boom and doing quite well.

Earlier we had been offered and had bought two-thirds of McNeill Drilling, another good business which fitted in with the construction industry. Hamish Pearson remained a one-third shareholder and the manager. We were still building in Invercargill and heavily involved in farming. We had bought Henderson Holms' property, another 686 acres, to add to the original farm we had bought from him, giving us a total of 1629 acres on that main block which we called Craigevar. With the 775 acres at Rocklands and the 886 acres in the bush at Progress Valley we had a large farming operation. We still had sawmilling, of course, and transport was humming along not too badly with a lot of diesel Macks replacing our petrol Internationals.

Our interests were extensive and we were still the same family business we had always been. But it was time for some soul-searching in that regard.

* * *

The early 1980s had resulted in lots of deals and acquisitions. In the short term, Ken and I had little to worry about. Longer term we had much to consider.

In 1982 Ken said the time had come for both of us to think about that. He had three sons. I had one. We presumed the boys would be interested in the business. But our observations had taught us that, traditionally, cousins did not get on very well running businesses. We pondered whether we should split up the business while the children were still at school. We could decide which pieces we wanted and try to make an even split, with neither owing the other any money.

We talked a lot and decided to go ahead. The family business would be split in two stages. Initially we divided off Niagara Sawmilling and R Richardson Ltd, which Ken took. I took Southern Transport and Allied Concrete, the latter at that stage operating in just Invercargill and Gore. It was, in fact, the original company because the other concrete interests were run under different names. In the last year we were together turnover was just under $17.5 million.

The following year we completed the split. Ken took the farming companies and McNeill Drilling while I took the shares in Timaru Readymix, Tregenzas, Purdues and Farrier Waimak.

After the first split, taking into account the companies I either owned or half-owned with Ken, turnover dropped back to $13.5 million. But after the second split, turnover increased to $15 million because of quite dramatic increases in business in two or three of those companies.

And so, in 1984, H W Richardson Group was formed. In 14 years we would increase that $15 million turnover tenfold.

The varying fleet colours of companies before the split. From left: McNeill Drilling, Niagara Sawmilling Company, J. H. Thomas & Co., Southern Transport and Allied Concrete.

8

THERE WAS NO TIME TO FEEL LONELY. As ever, business depended on taking opportunities and, while I could plan for the future on the basis of what I knew and expected, I had no crystal ball on where those opportunities would come from. Therefore I was amazed to discover that our largest expansions would be by courtesy of my business opposition. First, a little history of that opposition is necessary.

Certified Concrete had pioneered readymix concrete in this country. Formed in 1938, it was the brainchild of Fletcher Construction. Sir James Fletcher 2 and, I believe, his father had travelled to America and seen readymix concrete in use there. They believed rightly there were openings for it in New Zealand. Fletchers in those days was basically a building contracting company and so, when they were approached by Winstones, who were major quarry operators and builders' supply merchants in Auckland, a 50/50 joint venture seemed sensible. Winstones saw an extension of their business in readymix and Fletchers were contractors. Certified Concrete was formed.

Sandy Cormack was hired to run the new company. He became in time the father of readymix concrete in this country. He was an engineer and the company was run by engineers who were very good at making concrete. They ran a business focused on quality and there's no doubt that New Zealanders as a whole should thank them for the high grade concrete that came to be expected, which was not always the case overseas.

But as time went on the business nature of Winstones and Fletchers began to change. Winstones was a building supply merchant and Fletchers moved more and more into that area until eventually they were in strong opposition to each other. That proved something of a dilemma for Certified Concrete, their joint venture. In the end they became incompatible as partners and didn't communicate well at all.

The engineers were left to run the company. Skilled at what they produced they may have been but they had a reasonably narrow focus on what they thought were suitable markets for readymix. They had started operations in Wellington, then in Auckland and over the years they spread into centres like Hawkes Bay, Palmerston North, Nelson, Christchurch and Invercargill. In all of those areas, apart from Auckland and Wellington, business traded as Certified Concrete (Invercargill) or wherever it happened to be. Locals, such as aggregate suppliers, hardware merchants or cement companies such as Golden Bay and Milburn, were encouraged to take shares. The only wholly owned companies were in the two main North Island centres, the other companies being partly owned but using the Certified name and fleet colours and with access to its expertise.

Certified Concrete reached the stage where it turned down opportunities to enter other markets. For instance the Timaru Readymix plant we had bought from Winstones in 1978 had been offered to Certified Concrete but they didn't think

Timaru was a suitable place for a readymix business because it was too small. Times were changing.

When Certified Concrete started business only central mix plants were constructed. Concrete was batched and mixed in the plant then tipped into the truck ready mixed. One feature of central mixing was that capital costs were higher, making it difficult for newcomers. It helped that Certified Concrete certainly had the engineers of New Zealand convinced that the only way to make readymix concrete was through central mix batching plants.

A year after Certified started in New Zealand, Readymix Concrete Ltd began in Australia, eventually being owned by Colonial Sugar Refineries, which for many years had a 25 percent interest in Fletchers.

However, in the mid-1950s, Pioneer Concrete, another Australian company established by an Italian immigrant called Tristin Antico, saw things differently. Pioneer established cheap dry batch plants and put owner drivers on the trucks, thereby keeping the capital cost down. The drivers normally owned the truck, while the company owned the mixer bowl and the plants.

The readymix concrete concept spread. An Australian, Bryan Kelman, went to England from that country to help establish Readymix there, and it grew so quickly that it was split off into a separate public company, its growth rate being on average a new concrete plant every 10 days for eight years. With a low capital cost, Pioneer also spread quite rapidly. It now has about 650 plants and Readymix about 1300.

Fletchers had co-operated in the establishment of Readymix and, I believe, lost a huge opportunity when the Australian company expanded to England. Once, at a meeting I attended, Bryan Kelman said Certified had been asked to go there with them but Winstones had turned it down.

How ironic that the two major companies in readymix concrete worldwide had come from Australia, which had been behind New Zealand in the beginning. But the speed with which the readymix business expanded around the world was an indication of how accepted that means of making and transporting concrete became.

The incompatible Fletchers and Winstones tried to split Certified Concrete, but both wanted Auckland, the major market. Eventually, according to the legend I heard, somebody forgot to renew the lease of the main Auckland plant which was on Winstones land, and Winstones told Certified to go. Then Fletchers went to Wellington and bought the only real aggregate company in the Capital called River Shingle and Sand 1935 Ltd. Having acquired that they told Certified Concrete they would not supply them with aggregate any more.

On this forlorn site, and against the advice of our competitors, we set to and established Capital Concrete.

A showdown was inevitable. It ended with Winstones taking the Auckland operation, an obvious step because they were the major quarry operators in that city at the time. Fletchers got the rest, with the exception of Nelson, which somehow fell between the cracks. They then tidied up the local shareholders in each of the different centres.

Fletchers also bought Firth Industries, a public company operating in Hamilton and Rotorua. It was bigger than Allied Concrete but not huge, and the name Firth was then added to all their concrete plants after the partitioning of Certified. Winstones carried on as Winstones in that it created a concrete division. It already had some plants trading as Winstones around Bay of Plenty and Hamilton.

This was all happening while we were building something of a chain ourselves, using different names. One day in 1985, while I was attending a readymix conference, one of the Firth hierarchy took me aside and said: "I just want you to know that we have ambitions to spread our network of concrete plants. We are undoubtedly going to bump into you because you obviously have ambitions in the same industry. We're going to have to put plants in centres that you're in and we're not."

This set me thinking. He wasn't threatening, but there was no mistaking what he was telling me. They were going to take us on.

I was still thinking about it when I got home. I confide in Shona totally and told her: "Well, the only way I can combat that is to do the opposite – put plants in some centres they're in that we're not in."

It seemed to me that our opportunities looked a lot better because they were in larger centres than we were, apart from Christchurch which was a dog market margin-wise anyway.

So my mind went beyond the South Island when searching for possible opportunities, crossed Cook Strait and concentrated on the capital city, Wellington. We bought our cement from Christchurch-based Milburn Cement, which owned a company with a quarry in Owhiro Bay, Wellington. Milburn was our main cement supplier, mainly because there was no alternative, but our relationship was always quite good. I telephoned and asked, if we were to put a readymix concrete plant in Wellington, would they supply us with aggregate. They said they would.

The next step was to buy a suitable section for a plant. I found one in Landfill Road, not far from a concrete plant that had gone broke and closed down. I didn't intend to follow the same fate but figured that zoning would not be a problem. The site was next to a hill so height restrictions wouldn't exist. A very co-operative Wellington City Council allowed us planning permission and work on the new plant began.

Not long afterwards, a Firth manager called. He, one of his regional managers and his boss would like to meet me in Christchurch. They didn't have time to meet me anywhere else. It would be in my interest to attend. I agreed, and we met at the Shakespeare Restaurant in Papanui Road.

The meal was very pleasant but I knew we were not there just to enjoy an evening of friendship and to encourage goodwill to all men. At the end the boss said: "They tell me you've bought a plot of land in Wellington."

"Yes," I said.

"Well, we just want to tell you that if you go ahead and build a readymix plant in Wellington we will break you. I don't mean in Wellington. We will break you."

He then proceeded to tell me they would slash the price of concrete in Invercargill and Christchurch and they would build plants in Gore and Timaru. On the day we started in Wellington they would slash the price of concrete by $15 a cubic metre.

"At the end," he said, "we'll see who has the deepest pockets."

"I'll have to think about this," I replied.

I returned home and said to Shona again: "Wellington must be the place to go because they certainly don't want me there."

* * *

We built the Capital Concrete plant ourselves. Helping pour concrete are (from left) Fin Pickering, Ted Wills, Bruce Campbell and Harold, who even spent his Saturday nights working on the job.

History was repeating itself. Even as a youngster our son, Harold, was extremely interested in the company. He loved trucks and he had a photographic memory. One Saturday afternoon he was with me in the office when I was sorting through some road tax matters. The trucks were lined up outside and I tried to recall the registration number of one particular vehicle.

"What's its number?" I asked Harold.

Straight away he rattled it off.

"How do you know that?" I asked, puzzled.

"I know all the registration numbers," he replied.

I couldn't believe it. I lined up my barely teenaged son against the wall so he couldn't see the vehicles outside and, picking trucks at random, asked him their registration numbers. He was right each time.

He was a better student than his father. He passed School Certificate. But, like me, he also left school at 16. This had not gone down well with his mother, a teacher, who wanted him to continue at school. While this was being debated I gave him a job for a week at Southland Concrete Products Ltd, a company we had bought in 1980 after Fred Blick, a local building contractor who had also been a director of McNeill Drilling, approached us. The company made fence posts and other concrete products, and was similar to what we did at Allied Gore.

"Take your bike, take your lunch," I ordered. Harold managed the work, with aching muscles and blistered hands. At the end of the week, I said to him: "You have two choices. You can go back to school or you can go back there and work for a year." Harold didn't hesitate. He went back to Southland Concrete Products.

Even drivers wondered why Harold was working there.

"I'm bringing him up," I would reply.

There he met Cyril Kettle, who would eventually work 50 years for the company. Cyril was a Labour man through and through and Harold was a young Tory. They argued politics all day, the older man and the youth. It did Harold the world of good because he saw the world through workers' eyes and he also earned their respect.

After his year there Harold worked in the laboratory at Allied Concrete and then drove trucks. When we started building in Wellington, Harold was keen to be involved. Our construction was under the direction of Ted Wills, who worked for

The main batching plant rises in Landfill Road, Wellington.

me for many years. Harold lived in a hut on the site, the only resident of Landfill Road. He had little idea of such things as cooking potatoes and regularly consulted his mother. Again it did him the world of good. He was not naturally practical but he had a good brain.

One Saturday night, a builder whose site was close by telephoned me in Invercargill.

"Is Harold your son?" he asked.

"Yes," I replied.

"Well," he said, "I don't know any other 19-year-old who would spend his Saturday night in Wellington tying wires for the foundation of a concrete plant for his old man who lives in Invercargill."

Much of the plant was built in Christchurch, shipped north and assembled. It was a real hands-on job. It might not have been the best plant in the world but it was good enough to do what we wanted to do. We chose a central mix plant because we feared our opposition would claim we were making inferior concrete if we had a dry batch plant.

In reality we didn't have that much money but those were easier times and our bank told us we should be spending. I don't think, however, our bankers expected us to spend quite as much as we did.

Our opposition in Wellington also included Winstones who, after the partitioning of Certified, were back in the capital through their purchase of another company called Gorrie Concrete. Further opposition came from a private company called Powell Brothers in Tawa.

Firth made one more attempt to head us off. One of the Firth representatives telephoned and asked: "Didn't you hear what we said at our meeting?"

"Yes, I heard."

"But you're still going ahead?"

"Yes, I'm still going ahead because what you told me you were going to do is easy to say but slightly more difficult to do."

To build the plant, of course, we had to get concrete from one of the opposition companies. Harold was on the job at Landfill Road when a concrete truck arrived one day. The driver looked at him and said: "You jokers won't last six months. This is our town. It always has been. It always will be."

"You could be right," said Harold, "but we have one thing going for us."

"What's that?" asked the driver, who wouldn't even get out of the truck to help unload the concrete.

"The opposition hires drivers like you."

Business began in Wellington under the brand of Capital Concrete and for the first few months there wasn't much love lost. Within a year, however, the market changed. Powell Bros sold out to Winstones. By that stage, Capital Concrete had 15 percent of the market and we were helped by our opposition. One of our first jobs was up a very steep hill, a job Winstones had refused to deliver to. The customer didn't know us but asked if we would do it. We did and subsequently sold that customer $600,000 worth of concrete in our first year.

There wasn't a great price war, in Wellington or elsewhere. Perhaps fortuitously, our swing into the Capital occurred at a time when work was booming. The 1987 sharemarket bust was not far away, but there was still enough work then for everybody.

* * *

It was flattering that the big boys were taking notice of our operations. I believed we were efficient and principled operators, offering good service and products, and our customers knew we would keep to our word. That's vitally important in any business and it helped us no end in our dealings.

Our largest competitors, however, had very deep pockets and we had to be wary. While Winstones and Fletchers had been battling against each other, we fitted comfortably into our markets and were happy to let them knock each other to their hearts' content. As a relatively small player, but one that was becoming noticed, we did reasonably well. But had they turned on us we could have been in trouble.

Then, to everyone's surprise, Fletchers took over Winstones and Golden Bay Cement, both at the same time, in an astonishing deal which had obviously been planned meticulously for some time by all three companies. That takeover changed forever the readymix industry in this country.

The Commerce Commission, a government body, was charged with overseeing takeovers and acquisitions in this country and ensuring true competitive forces remained intact. Monopolies were to be discouraged. Having seen what it had

Capital Concrete completed and ready for action.

Speirs Concrete, Levin, which we bought in 1990, had candy-coloured trucks.

allowed in the past, apparently without being aware of the consequences, I have to admit that I had little faith in the commission.

In this instance the commission had previously declined Fletchers permission to take over Winstones and therefore had been outwitted by some very clever people who knew the law and how to get around the commission's ruling. Golden Bay Cement was owned by the Blue Circle Group in England, which wanted to pull out of New Zealand entirely. To do that it needed to sell Golden Bay Cement. At that stage Brierley Investments Ltd controlled Winstones and they desperately wanted to sell it to Fletchers, which was considered the only likely buyer. Fletchers could see advantages because Winstones had good resources and many of its activities were complementary to what they did.

The commission obviously saw nothing amiss when both Brierley and Fletchers sought to buy up to 100 percent of Golden Bay Cement because it approved both applications. Under New Zealand law at that time, a company owning 50 percent or more of another company did not need approval from the commission to do any further deals involving that company. So Brierley Investments bought 50 percent of Golden Bay Cement and Fletchers bought the other half. This would not have been what the commission expected. It would have expected the two companies to battle it out for control of Golden Bay.

A further surprise was in store. Brierley Investments sold Winstones to Golden Bay Cement. No permission was needed because BIL owned half or more of both companies. And once Golden Bay owned Winstones, Fletchers, which had previously gained permission to buy up to 100 percent of the cement company, took it over completely. Before the Commerce Commission knew what had happened, Fletchers owned Winstones.

What a clever deal, I thought at the time, and my initial reaction was one of anxiety. This would truly be one large competitor with a lot of resources that could do us considerable damage.

In fact, the opposite happened. Before long we were confronted with expansion opportunities throughout the North Island.

Fletchers knew the commission would not be happy and moved immediately to sell operations where they thought they might be accused of running monopolies. One such area was readymix concrete in certain locations, including Wellington. When we started there, there were four operators. Suddenly, there were two. We had 15 percent of the market, Firths had 85 percent. Fletchers knew they would be frowned upon by the commission, which has indicated its dislike for any operator to have more than 70 percent of a market.

Fletchers also knew that Milburn Cement, which was controlled by the Holderbank Group, a massive Swiss cement manufacturing, readymix and aggregate company with worldwide interests, would be extremely nervous. Milburn made about half of New Zealand's cement and Golden Bay the other half. With Golden Bay owned by Fletchers, and with its links to Firth, Stresscrete, concrete masonry, retail chain Placemakers and other operations, they held a large percentage of sales in what could be seen as a captive market. Milburn, on the other hand, had no downstream operations.

The Swiss suggested to Milburn in New Zealand that they get into the readymix business and quickly. Another complicating factor was that Firth was their largest cement customer and bought a large percentage of their production, making Milburn extremely vulnerable.

Fletchers well understood this situation, of course, and approached me with an offer. They knew our market percentage and they knew we bought cement from Milburn. They proposed they sell their Powells plant, offering it both to Milburn and us, and may the better company win.

This is going to be interesting, I thought, because if we didn't buy it, we would have two opposition companies, and both were cement producers. We had to buy our cement from one or the other and we could have been squeezed. Yet we couldn't outbid Milburn because they had far more money. I wasn't sure what to do.

Milburn, it turned out, came to us. They were keen to get into the readymix business. They proposed they buy us out, completely.

"No," I said, "we're not for sale."

This was the second time in just over a year that I had been asked to sell out. After the partitioning of Certified Concrete, Winstones had approached us with a similar proposition. Their area consisted of only the Auckland, Waikato and Bay of Plenty regions and they had no national geographical spread. They were particularly keen to get into the South Island. I turned them down, largely because Harold was keen to get into the business and I was far from ready to sell. I gave Milburn the same explanation.

Not long afterwards, a Milburn representative returned.

"There must be something we can do," he said. "Will you sell your Wellington operation?"

"I've just spent a lot of money building it," I replied. "I've lost $500,000 in the first 12 to 18 months of trading getting it on the road and having a bit of a battle on prices so I'm not ready to toss it in at this stage."

"Well, come back with some sort of offer," he said.

"Okay," I said, "you buy Powells plant off Fletchers for whatever it costs, I don't care. Then I'll put my plant in and we'll go into a 50/50 venture."

I added: "But I want my plant plus a cash figure." I felt my plant was worth more than Powells. Fortunately they agreed and we formed a 50/50 company called Allied Milburn, with a board of four – two from Allied Concrete and two from Milburn. Another stipulation was that I would have management control. They agreed to that as well. The extra money I spent buying a share in Owhiro Bay Quarries Ltd with Milburn and Fulton Hogan.

We were slightly less formal than Milburn. One of their managers was interested in how we operated.

"How do you handle your capex?" he asked.

"Capex?" I deadpanned.

"Capital expenditure. For buying new trucks and so on," he said.

"What do you do?" I asked.

"We have a manual," he replied.

"Well, I go out and kick the tyres and say, this one's shot let's get another," I explained.

"I had a horrible feeling you were going to say that," the manager replied.

Yet I wasn't the only one with an off-beat sense of humour. In Wellington we had to bring the teams from Capital Concrete and Powell together, and we decided a barbecue at Powell's plant in Tawa seemed like a good idea.

The invitations went out and, on the day, we met at Powell's yard. When we got there the men from Wellington hadn't turned up so we waited. Suddenly an immaculate limousine drove into the yard and out poured the Capital Concrete team.

"Did that look impressive enough?" one of them asked me.

"It looked very impressive," I said. "What's the idea?"

"We just thought we'd let those guys know who's taking over who," he replied. "We were going to hire a helicopter but we couldn't all get into one, and we couldn't afford to hire two."

* * *

In 1988, just a month or so after we put Allied Milburn together, Firth approached us and offered us three plants in Rotorua, Tauranga and Taupo because they also had an effective monopoly with two plants in each market. We were moving up the country faster than my mind had contemplated.

We placed those plants under the same umbrella and traded as Central Concrete. Their markets were depressed but slowly they picked up and turned into reasonable businesses.

Then in 1990 we were offered Speirs Concrete in Levin, which gave us a plant in that town and a just-commissioned operation in Paraparaumu. Gold Coast Concrete in nearby Otaki followed which gave us a strong presence in the growing Horowhenua/Kapiti Coast areas. In 1991 we procured Waikato Readymix in Hamilton. Redi-crete in Palmerston North was next, and a small plant in Foxton joined our stable in 1992.

The South Island was not neglected. We bought Ashby Concrete in Christchurch from Bitumix, which was really BP Oil – a bigger deal and a good operation. Then we returned to the lower North Island to buy Wainui Readymix in Wainuiomata

Gold Coast Concrete trucks were bright yellow, perhaps reflecting Otaki sunshine. We bought the company in 1990.

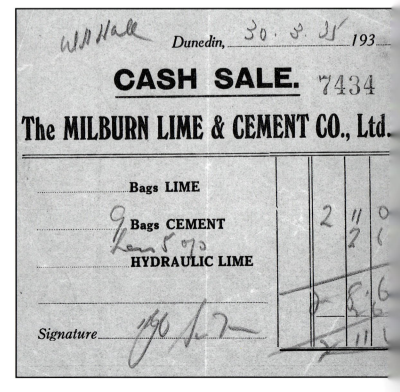

Right: Our relationship with Milburn has come a long way since my grandfather made this purchase in 1935, to the stage where we are now spending in excess of 25 million dollars a year with them.

Waikato Ready Mix trucks from Hamilton had two-tone bowls. We bought the company in 1991.

and Gorrie Concrete in Upper Hutt. Bruntons, also in that city, was next. After that, we started a joint venture in Masterton.

We had also been buying under the Allied Concrete Ltd umbrella. That included Timaru Readymix in 1978 and Farriers in 1984. We were also in partnership with Fulton Hogan in our 50 percent interest with Daveys Concrete, Balclutha, from 1983 to 1988 when we dissolved that by selling Daveys back to Fulton Hogan. At the same time we bought Ashburton Concrete, which Daveys had bought in the meantime from Burnetts. We also took a quarter interest in Queenstown Concrete in 1988 through a joint venture we had called Allied FH Ltd, which owned half of the business, Northern Southland Transport Holdings owning the other half.

One year later we had moved into Marlborough, buying Fulton Hogan's shares in Marlborough Readymix and buying out the other partners a year or so later. We went into partnership with Fulton Hogan in Nelson in 1990, buying the company which had slipped through the net in the clean-up with Fletchers and Winstones, trading as Certified Concrete (Nelson) Ltd. That partnership lasted about two years, when we bought out Fulton Hogan's half-share. In 1990 we bought Shiel Concrete from Palmers in Dunedin, opening a presence in that city.

Yet the company which undertook probably the biggest job we have ever done was Lloyds Concrete in Alexandra. Ken and I had bought a 60 percent interest in 1986 and eventually bought out the Lloyd family. Then I bought out Ken's share, and it became a branch of Allied Concrete Ltd.

Stabilisation tunnels were needed for the much-troubled Clyde Dam project and we poured something like 70,000 cubic metres of concrete down holes and into tunnels. Originally, having won the tender, we did the job from Alexandra because nobody knew how much concrete was going to be required. Those behind the project just started ordering concrete.

So our trucks roared up and down the road between Alexandra and Clyde, and the business grew until those trucks were travelling 1000km a day and working 24 hours around the clock. We had never struck the likes of it before. We reached the stage where we decided to build a plant on the Clyde site, which cut down travelling time considerably. The job turned out to be huge, and it only happened because we were in the right place at the right time with the right price.

This period of rapid expansion was no haphazard strategy. We were in the mood to expand and we looked for plants which had a reasonable volume of work

Pouring concrete for stablisation tunnels for the Clyde Dam project proved a huge project for Lloyd's Concrete, of Alexandra, in which we had taken a controlling interest in 1986, lately buying it completely.

Getting the concrete to the required spot was not always easy on the Clyde Dam stablilisation project. In this instance, we had to barge the concrete across the newly-formed Lake Dunstan.

which would spread our network. We looked at location and potential, rather than equipment. Sometimes we approached a company, sometimes companies approached us. Nearly all of the transactions were straightforward deals, except for one in the lower North Island.

We were buying the plant through Allied Milburn. We did the deal, and Milburn's representative gave the owner a deposit cheque of $50,000. A couple of days later, his accountant telephoned.

"We have a slight problem," he said.

"What's the problem?" I asked.

"Well, this guy's signed an unconditional contract of sale with Firth."

"He never told us that."

There didn't seem to be much we could do if that was the case so I asked the accountant to send us back our $50,000.

"I can't do that," he said.

"Why's that?" I asked.

"Because he used your $50,000 to pay his overdue account with Golden Bay Cement."

I laughed. I don't know why because half of it was my money. But I could imagine the faces at Milburn when they learned their deposit had gone to pay off their competitor. We talked to Firth and, fortunately, they backed off and the deal went ahead.

* * *

That was a business problem that had been quite easily resolved. We thought we had a deal, it didn't turn out to be as straightforward as we thought, but we settled it quite quickly. Business life tends to be like that. Sometimes, however, those difficulties can turn very sour indeed.

After we had bought Tregenzas, we bought 27 acres at Washdyke, on the outskirts of Timaru, from the major stock and station agency, Wrightsons, which was part of the Fletcher Challenge Group then. Wrightsons had inherited the property from Dalgety's when they took over that stock and station agency and it contained some quite large storage sheds.

About 1987 we were approached by a company called Duraphos New Zealand Ltd, a subsidiary of Wrightsons, which had been formed to go into the fertiliser business using a fertiliser from Israel. The Duraphos people asked if we would cart the fertiliser from the wharves at Timaru, store it in our sheds on the Washdyke property, then reload it for their customers. When we agreed they also asked us if we could extend the sheds so that they could hold 15,000 tonnes. We did that and 13,000 tonnes of the fertiliser were soon in our store.

We had done all this on the basis of a verbally agreed deal and terms of contract had been written up. We had signed and sent it to Wrightsons head office in Wellington. But we never received it back.

Then, to our surprise, we heard Duraphos had sold its fertiliser interests to Ravensdown, the Dunedin-based fertiliser company. We quickly asked where that left us. The Duraphos people said they would look after us and come to see us when they had time. I felt that they would be more inclined to look after us while we held their 13,000 tonnes of fertiliser and told our people in Timaru not to let it go.

I flew to Wellington and met one of the Wrightsons people. We discussed the issue, determined what would be a fair outcome in terms of what we had put into helping them establish themselves, and shook hands on it. The next day I was amazed when the man I had done this deal with telephoned to say he had been thinking about it overnight and the deal was off. Not even when I pointed out that we had shaken hands on it would he change his mind.

I told him we would not release the fertiliser and would sue them. Sue away, the Wrightsons man said. Duraphos only had a paid-up capital of $10,000 so that wouldn't get us far, he challenged.

In the event, Duraphos was first to court in Timaru to get us to release the fertiliser. Our own legal advice was that we would lose because no contract had been signed by both parties. But going to court allowed us to make a strong point to the Judge – that we weren't impressed that a company as big as Wrightsons could let this happen and hide behind a small subsidiary. Not unexpectedly, the Judge said he would have to find against us and order us to release the fertiliser. He wasn't impressed with Wrightsons either and ordered that it be enjoined in any legal claim that we might pursue.

In due course we proceeded with our own legal action for $1 million which seemed a nice round figure for the costs we had incurred on their behalf. Months

In 1994, we bought King Concrete in Auckland, and we had reached New Zealand's largest market.

went by, and I came back from my Christmas holiday to find a very thick legal brief on my desk. A hearing had been set down for the following May.

I'm sick of this, I thought. It was a waste of time and money and I couldn't believe that the senior management staff at either Fletcher Challenge or Wrightsons would condone what had happened. I had met Fletchers' Chief Executive Hugh Fletcher briefly and, on the spur of the moment, telephoned him in Auckland. His secretary said he wasn't available but what was the call about. I told her and then said we had had a lot of dealings with Fletchers in the concrete industry recently and I would be surprised if he knew what was going on, and even more surprised if he approved. She promised to tell him of my concerns.

The very next day I had a telephone call from Rick Bettle, chief executive of Wrightsons. He told me he'd been told to get to Invercargill and sort out our problem. I told him I'd be going to Wellington in a day or so, so I'd save him the cost of an air fare. We set up a meeting.

Bettle, when I met him in his large office in downtown Wellington, was straightforward. His legal people had told him they had no liability. I agreed with him, but morally, I told him, they did. He asked me what we'd settle for. I said I'd let him know.

I telephoned him back on a Wednesday. "We'll settle for $440,000 plus GST," I said.

"You'll have the cheque by Friday," he said.

In the end, Fletcher Challenge did the honourable thing but it had taken 18 costly months to sort out. And, as often happens after such battles, there were a couple of humorous consequences.

After the fertiliser had gone Wrightsons hired the sheds to store wool in. And, later, Rick Bettle came to live in Southland as chief executive of the Alliance Group which, at the time, was in financial difficulties.

One day, I saw him at Invercargill Airport and went over to ask if he remembered me. He did, recalling our meeting and what had happened. He left me with no doubt that the Duraphos incident was one of the silliest Wrightsons had got itself into.

* * *

By this time, our own business had grown to the point where it was all a bit confusing. We had 15 different names in our readymix operation. We were trading as Allied Concrete, Shiel Concrete, Timaru Readymix, Ashburton Concrete, Farrier Waimak Ltd, Rangiora Readymix, Marlborough Readymix Concrete, Certified Concrete (Nelson) Ltd and Lloyds Concrete in Alexandra. That was just in the South Island.

In the North Island, we had Capital Concrete in Wellington, Speirs Concrete in Paraparaumu, Palmerston North and Levin, Foxton Concrete in that town, Gold Coast Concrete in Otaki, Central Concrete in the Bay of Plenty and Waikato Readymix in Hamilton.

We were competing with Firth which had one name nationally and I decided those companies we owned entirely should trade as Allied Concrete Ltd. I asked the people at Milburn if they had any thoughts on how they wanted to trade the Allied Milburn operations but they had no bright ideas. After some discussion we decided all our operations should trade as Allied Concrete, even though they were under two sets of ownership, and Harold would run the two companies.

Our next step logically was Auckland, the country's largest market. There was little sense in having a chain of readymix concrete plants which began in Invercargill and ended in Hamilton when the largest concrete market in the country was just up the road. But for various reasons, including their ownership of readymix plants in the Waikato and Auckland, Milburn was not interested in any further move north.

One of their executives, who was on the board of Allied Milburn at the time, told me: "If you want to go to Auckland, go on your own."

Moving into Auckland was another defining step in the company's history. In 1994, at the annual conference of the Readymix Association, I told a Firth representative that we intended to move into Auckland. Firth representatives came back to us shortly afterwards and asked if we would be interested in buying half of King Concrete at Manukau, which they owned 50/50 with Downer Mining. I said we wouldn't be interested in buying half of it, but we would be interested in buying all of it.

Firth inherited its half through their takeover of Winstones and they eventually managed to do a deal with Downer Mining to get them out. Then they offered us a deal where we bought half of the company and ran it for two years and, at the end of that period, they sold us the other half.

That led us into Auckland. King Concrete was a reasonably sized operation based in Manukau, with a good fleet of trucks and plant and quite a high profile in the marketplace. We had not been there long, however, when it became obvious we needed a second plant on the North Shore because a significant percentage of our concrete was going there. We had learned quickly the realities of Auckland traffic. Carting concrete from Manukau across the Harbour Bridge early in the morning was fine, but returning for a second load resulted in trucks being tied up for long periods in traffic.

We decided to build on the North Shore, near Albany, bought the land and received permission to proceed. But there's always someone who doesn't like progress and one objector managed to stall us for 18 months. Eventually we overcame all the hurdles and built our new plant.

Not surprisingly our Auckland branch, with 28 trucks, is our biggest. It also wins big jobs, including concrete for the much-publicised Mercury Energy tunnel, and pouring 18,000 cubic metres of concrete to extend the runway and airport tarmac for the numerous jets bearing international leaders for the APEC conference in September 1999.

It was a marvellous period in our history and one which gave me considerable satisfaction and pride. We had grown with amazing speed and, despite the spread of our operations, we managed to run them well, thanks largely to knowledgeable staff who knew the business and their customers. While many of the opportunities came about through Firth having two plants in the same centres after the Winstones takeover, others came about because smaller operators perceived the business was going to get harder.

Perhaps it was, but from our viewpoint it certainly became more exciting.

9

ALL THAT EXPANSION HAD OCCURRED NATURALLY and in an orderly manner. We had a major partner in Milburn admittedly but Allied Concrete's own expansion was in itself proof that our company was performing well enough to finance our expansion.

Bringing trucks into line for fleet photographs is a habit of transport companies but this line-up of the Farrier Waimak fleet came about through a remarkable amount of effort. It was taken on Saturday, September 14, 1957. The drivers ended their day at the plant, then the dozers and other machinery were brought in. The company boasted that all but a few of the trucks were ready for the road again by 8am on Monday.

I could afford to reflect and smile at how we had not always been in such a position. Compounding that enjoyment was the fact that the Richardsons had not always had the happiest of relationships with financial institutions. We recognised we needed them, although sometimes their lack of generosity left us wondering. Sometimes, I'm sure, those institutions wondered if they needed us at all, but we certainly ended up to their benefit as well. The Richardsons were used to adversity, and financial institutions were, in a sense, fair game.

My father's relationship with financiers had been interesting. Like his father before him, who used to say that a banker was a person who lent you his umbrella on a fine day, and wanted it back as soon as it started to rain, he was cynical of bankers and professional people generally.

Three generations of Richardsons would tell the story of the contractor who died and went to Heaven where he noticed that contractors and workers were lean

and hungry while bankers, lawyers and accountants were well fed. The contractor wondered about that, until meal-time. Everyone was issued with a long-handled wooden spoon which was strapped to their forearms. To feed themselves they dipped the spoon into a large bowl of stew. But because the spoon was long and strapped to their forearms, they couldn't get the spoons into their mouths. The contractor noticed how other contractors held the laden spoon up and let the food run down the handle, so they could lick it off their arms. Then he looked at the bankers, lawyers and accountants. They sat side by side and allowed the next person to eat from their spoons.

"Just like on Earth," said the contractor, "they're all feeding off each other."

Sometimes, subterfuge had been used. In difficult Niagara days in 1948 my father and Jim Farrelly had gone to one of Invercargill's banks to try to raise £2000. Dad was there because Grandad was overseas. Farrelly presented a list of equipment they were prepared to put up as security. The banker seemed reasonably impressed.

When they left the banker to think about the loan Farrelly said to my father: "Drive me round to the insurance company. I want to put some insurance cover on that equipment." Two weeks later my father learned an insurance representative had turned up at the mill with a list of equipment that he wanted to examine. Dad referred the matter to Farrelly and some time later he received a phone call from the banker.

"Tell me," he said, "that list of equipment. Does it exist?"

"You'll have to ask Farrelly," said my father, "but please don't confuse Niagara Sawmilling with R Richardson Ltd." It must have dawned on the banker he'd had the wool pulled over his eyes, but by that time Farrelly had his £2000.

After Dad had bought out his father and Niagara, and money and profitability presented huge difficulties, a banker called him in.

"For the size of your business and the amount of assets you have tied up you're not getting a big enough return on your capital invested."

Dad replied: "From where I'm sitting it's not looking too bad. I've actually got only £75 invested because that's all I started with. No one has given me anything since."

I suppose it's fair to say that our business today came from that same £75. No one ever gave us any money, it all came out of the business.

On yet another interview with the banker, who was at least 10 years older than my father, Dad said to him: "I've got quite a lot of assets. If you were me, would you swap your assets for mine?"

"Of course not," the banker replied. "You have a lot more assets than I've got."

Dad looked at him. "And you're sitting there telling me I'm not doing any good."

My father was with the Commercial Bank of Australia for many years through some difficult times. We had never let them down but the bank obviously did not have much faith in us. Dad at one stage had organised a facility for $125,000 and, although the business grew many times in turnover, the bank would not allow us any more.

One time Ken was heading to Wellington.

"Why don't you go and see those jokers in the Head Office of the CBA, tell them what we're doing and see if you can get anywhere with them," I suggested.

Ken duly did and met a banker who told him he considered the Commercial Bank of Australia had more money invested in our business than we did and therefore he would do nothing about changing the facility.

We decided to change to the Bank of New South Wales. We prepared our case, saying we would move if they gave us double the facility, or $250,000. The Wales turned us down. Money was tight at the time and they conceded we didn't look too bad, but they couldn't front with the money. So we remained with the CBA.

Mum and Dad had been on a bus trip through Europe and the Mediterranean where they met an Australian, Keith Bennell, and his wife. As so often happens when such tours near their end, they said to them: "If you're ever in New Zealand, look us up."

In 1975, Keith Bennell and his wife duly arrived in New Zealand, and stayed with Mum and Dad for a couple of nights. I helped to show them around.

"Who do you bank with?" he asked Dad, who told him.

"Why don't you go to the Wales?" Keith Bennell asked.

Dad told him we had tried but the Wales did not want us.

Bennell then asked to look over our balance sheet and Dad agreed. The next day I showed him our farms and operations. At Rocklands Farm he pointed to the house and asked: "Is there a phone in that house?"

"Yes," I said.

"Do you mind if I make a toll call?"

"Not at all," I said, and he was gone for about 10 minutes.

When he returned, he said: "You and your brother have a meeting with the Invercargill manager of the Wales tomorrow morning at 9 o'clock."

"Have we?" I asked.

"Go and tell them what you want," Keith Bennell said. "I think you'll get a more favourable response."

The next morning Ken and I went to meet Frank Porter.

"I don't know who your mate is," said Porter, "but my boss knows him well and holds him in high regard. I've been told that if you guys want to shift to us, we'll double your limit [which was the $250,000 we were asking for] and will take you forthwith."

It was as easy as that. We couldn't believe our luck. Keith Bennell turned out to be a partner in a large Australian accounting firm who did a lot of financial work for the Bank of New South Wales.

A bigger surprise came when we went to the manager of the Commercial Bank of Australia.

"We've come to tell you we're leaving your bank," I said. "After all these years we have a better offer."

Ken and I did not know what to expect, but we did not expect the manager to say: "It's all very well for you, you can get out of it. If it wasn't for my superannuation, I'd be out of here too." That was how much regard he had for his employers.

Not long afterwards the Bank of New South Wales had a new manager called Jack Linklater. One day he came to see us and our operations. He was wearing a lapel badge with eight letters on it, YDGBSOYA. Obviously, it wasn't a Rotary badge. Finally, I could contain my curiosity no longer.

"What does your badge mean?"

"It's a very simple philosophy I have in banking," he explained. "You Don't Get Business Sitting On Your Arse." He was the first bank manager I could recall who came to visit us to try to understand what we were about and what we did. As a result, we got on well with Jack.

Over the years, we had also dealt solely with one finance company. In 1970, when we were forming United Plant Hire with Gordon Hoffman, we were selling the large NCK crane we had built while buying a new Coles hydraulic crane at a cost of $47,000, a

Transporting prefabricated houses could have its challenges. This particular house was to be transported up the Crown Range with its notorious zig-zags, before the road was sealed.

Harold's early interest in trucks was such that he memorised the registration numbers. But, like me, he also had fond memories of the trucks he rode in as a child. One of his favourites was the Leyland Crusader, which had cost a very expensive $35,000 in its time. At the end of its working life, he encouraged me to have it restored and we are pictured together as it was about to enter the truck museum.

large amount of money in those days. Buying the new crane was very much dependent on selling the old one for $35,000 to a Whakatane firm, who also dealt with the same finance company.

We went to the finance company presuming two deals could be arranged virtually as one. But a representative of the finance company came back to us, saying they would finance the deal on our new crane but they would not finance selling the old crane to the Whakatane company.

"They are unreliable and we won't touch them" he said.

That's odd, I thought. They did not strike me as unreliable. It was an old, well-established firm, having been in business since the 1920s. I had a bank report done on the company, not that bank reports were worth much, but it confirmed my feelings about the company. It said they were reliable and had never been known to enter into deals they could not complete.

I went back to the finance company and asked them to check. They would not change their minds. I then asked them to ask their principals to reconsider. The answer was the same. Gordon Hoffman broke the impasse by approaching his finance company, which agreed to finance both deals.

We eventually found out that the Whakatane company had been looking at a new crane as well and the finance company we were dealing with also financed the agent for the new crane. The agents knew about our deal and told the finance company not to touch the old crane, thus trying to spike the deal so they could sell the new one. When I discovered this I took the greatest pleasure in telling the finance company I would never deal with them again.

When Ken and I split the business in 1984, we agreed we would walk away not owing each other any money. When we were together we would finance many deals by hire purchasing our equipment and keeping any cash we accumulated in readiness for any deals that came along. That meant if a deal came our way we could write a cheque rather than have to go through the rigmarole of offering money subject to finance and then having to wait until that was cleared.

It was a lot easier and far more advantageous to put in an unconditional offer and say: "Yes, we'll buy it, here's the money."

We had bought all our plant on hire purchase and, in the split, I had said I wanted all the trucks and transport and readymix interests. To get the assets somewhere close to 50/50 when we split, Ken had to take all the cash and I had to take all the debt. That meant I had a lot of hire purchase payments, which wasn't comfortable when I didn't have the money in the bank to cover those commitments. I had 18 months of hire purchase debt running at about $100,000 a month to pay off, a total of $1.8 million, although eventually we paid it off without missing a payment.

One day in 1985, the Ford dealer in Timaru telephoned me and said: "I've got a buyer for a Dodge concrete truck and I'll sell you a new one."

We had a Dodge concrete truck which was getting a bit tired and they were quite hard to sell. I said I would think about it but I didn't want any more hire purchase debt. I already had enough.

We dealt with a particular finance company so I telephoned and asked what sort of deal I would get if I sold the Dodge, gave that cash to the finance company, and then made no payments for 12 months on the new truck, after which I would pay off the concrete truck within 12 months. That would not exceed another principle I had committed myself to. I would not buy on hire purchase if payments stretched longer than two years. By that time I felt if you couldn't handle such arrangements in that period then you probably shouldn't be getting into them.

The finance company came up with an arrangement which I accepted and I telephoned the Ford dealer in Timaru to say the deal was on. He could take the new truck to the paint shop. We were in business.

About 4.30 that same afternoon, the finance company's representative telephoned to say: "I'm sorry, I can't get out this afternoon to sign the deal. Will it be okay if I make it first thing in the morning?" I agreed.

He was a man I had signed many deals with and he duly arrived at 8.30am the next day.

"There's only one slight hitch," he said.

"What's that?" I asked.

"We had an interest rate movement overnight," he said. "Everything signed up from this morning has a higher interest rate."

"But I did this deal yesterday," I protested. "It was you who put off coming out because you were busy."

"I know, but there's nothing I can do about it."

"Well, you'd better ring your boss and explain the circumstances because I've paid you millions over the last year or two and on principle I think this is wrong.

The purchase of Herberts Transport of Edendale in 1993, with Jim Dynes, of Tapanui, proved a good one. Spraying whey from the Edendale Dairy Factory on to paddocks was one of its business operations.

It won't be much interest [it was actually $900] but in principle, it's not right."

He went away and returned.

"They won't move up north," he said. "You'll have to pay."

"Okay," I said, "give me the document. I'll pay it."

As I handed it back, I told him: "Take a good look at it. It's the last you'll see with my signature on it."

"Why's that?" he asked.

"You just took $900 off me that I didn't actually owe you. We did a deal yesterday at 2 o'clock. You were coming out, you were held up. I pay the $900. That's not the way life is."

I refused to deal with them again. Head office representatives came to see me, offering to take me for lunch.

"What have we got to do to get your business back?" they asked.

"I won't deal with you because you owe me $900," I would reply.

Five years later a new manager, an Australian who had obviously heard the story, came to see me. I repeated: "You guys owe me $900."

"You're not going to deal with us again until we give you the $900, are you," he said.

"No," I replied.

The next day, a cheque for $1000 arrived in the mail. It had taken five years for that company to get the message and they had missed out on a lot of business in the meantime because of their stupidity.

I'd also found banks could be inconsistent. Just before we developed into Wellington about 1986, our banker telephoned (the Bank of New South Wales had become Westpac by this stage) and said we weren't expanding much. We should be spending more money.

"Just get going, we'll back you," he said.

Once we started building we used all our cash and needed a little more so we took up his offer. Then he was transferred. A new manager came to see us and said the bank required a formal application for the extra money we would need to complete the Wellington plant. We duly did so, he sent it away and it came back saying it had been turned down. The bank also said we had no right to expand our business outside our normal area of operations.

I asked the manager what his Head Office meant by that. Did they mean geographical areas, or areas of expertise?

"I don't know what they mean by that," he replied.

"So why put it in if you don't know what it means?" I asked.

I took a dim view of all this because the bank knew what we were doing, or their previous manager did. So I wrote back saying if they wanted to close the account they should let me know by return mail and I would make other arrangements. They backed off quickly. In fact I had not seen a banker so keen to meet me.

When we were buying more and more plants the bank became more and more institutionalised and we never knew who we would be dealing with. Once the bank asked me to sign a personal guarantee because of our exposure, not that they were particularly worried. They considered me a sole trader, which was true, but when our shareholders' funds reached a certain level, which they nominated, they would review the requirement for a personal guarantee. I had always said I would back the company to the limit so that did not worry me.

After the 1987 sharemarket crash I saw banks do things to people that I didn't much like. I felt they acted in haste and wound up some people who didn't deserve it. At the same time they had lent money to some individuals they should have stayed away from.

I was thinking of this lack of fair play at the time of our annual review. I looked again at the letter the bank had sent, consulted the balance sheet and found our shareholders' funds exceeded the nominated limit by several million dollars. So I asked the bank to remove the personal guarantee.

Locally the bank indicated that was not a problem. But in Head Office they refused. Eventually, I spoke to a Head Office official.

"What's the story here?" I asked.

"There's no way we're going to remove the personal guarantee because it's a rule of the bank that there must be a personal guarantee for an account of your size for a sole trader," the official said.

"When have the rules changed?" I asked.

"They have never changed. That's always been the case," he replied.

"Either the rules have changed or, when you wrote this letter to me in the first place, you were telling lies because it says that when the shareholders' funds exceeded the figure you nominated you would review the need for a personal guarantee. So what you're telling me is that you had no intention of reviewing the need."

The official didn't know what to say about that but I was so angry I tried to transfer our account to another bank. We managed to get just as good an agreement without a personal guarantee but that bank wanted to do an annual audit because they didn't know us. We'd never had such an audit and it looked like being expensive and messy.

Fortunately the manager of a different Westpac division heard of our dilemma, looked at our accounts and decided his division would take our account without an audit or a personal guarantee. We changed from one division of Westpac to another. I would have loved dearly to tell the bank where to go but it was simpler to stay where we were. We've got on well since.

This is what was left of our Ford concrete truck after the Opuha dam burst. It took us weeks to find the bowl.

Macks were becoming predominant in our fleet by the early 1980s.

THE READYMIX CONCRETE BUSINESS had grown at an unbelievable rate. But we were also adding elsewhere to our business, as well as making changes of direction.

We had expanded Southern Transport a great deal over the years. With our 33 trucks in the early 1970s we carted a lot of gravel, livestock and other farming goods, along with more and more industrial work and logs. Then, in 1979, I had analysed the company's business – what we did well and what was profitable – and I had to admit that Dave King was right all those years earlier when he said the rural runs we had were too short. We were, in fact, too close to the freezing and fertiliser works near Invercargill. Further, the city had spread and many farms had been divided into lifestyle blocks and we were trying to service these small holdings as well. I ran through the figures and discovered that 50 percent of our administration was servicing about 15 percent of our turnover.

It was time for Southern Transport to get out of rural transport and I put that division on the market in October 1979. It was almost sold when the prospective buyer backed out. But the economics of selling out remained compelling so I gave our clients three months notice and then sold off the equipment that had serviced that sector. In fact I received $30,000 more than I was going to get selling it as a going concern, so the prospective purchaser had done me a favour. We had been in that type of business for 19 years but changing times meant it was time for us to move on.

In 1983 another opportunity in a different area arose. That year some of the shareholders of Gore Services Ltd, the agent for Mobil fuel in that town, approached me to change our fleet to Mobil and join their company. I had always been loyal to Caltex since their assistance to us in the early days and had never used any other fuel. But Caltex was not interested in an agency deal and, on inquiry, volunteered that they thought any moral obligation we might feel to them had been well and truly repaid, which I thought was very decent of them. I agreed to change Allied Gore to Mobil and that allowed me to become a small shareholder in Gore Services.

Gore Services had been established in 1956 by Tom MacLean, a farmer and car, truck and farm machinery dealer in the town. He had also started importing a re-refined American engine oil. As well, with some others, he ran a finance company called Reliable Finance, which had financed many carriers and others into business when they had found it difficult to get finance from other more traditional sources. Tom gambled on the man, and he was usually right. Such people then felt a loyalty to him and they were the natural target for his re-refined engine oil. Before long he was selling a lot of oil, christening it Mactrol – Mac from his own name and -trol from the well-known Castrol brand.

One day, two men from Mobil had come to him. They had noted they were not selling much oil around Gore, thanks mainly to him. They suggested it would be better if he were their agent. A few hours later two men from Europa arrived and made a similar offer. Tom had no affiliation to any oil company but, because Mobil had arrived first, he entered into a business arrangement to be the agent for their oil and fuels in Gore.

It was a relatively simple operation. Fuel was carted from the port of Bluff by tanker and put in large tanks in Gore. From those it was distributed to various carriers and farmers. Tom was the agent, owned the tanker and delivered the fuel. He was then able to contact the mates he had financed into business and sold re-refined oil to and suggest they change to Mobil fuel. That way there would be a base turnover for the business, a base load for the truck delivering the fuel, and he would sell his friends shares in the business. Thus Gore Services Ltd was formed and run successfully, with Tom holding a 26 percent controlling interest.

By 1983, however, Tom was getting older and the company was looking for a new chairman. But none of the shareholders either wanted the job or would agree to have any of the other shareholders as chairman. I was dubious. I knew all the shareholders. I agreed to join, only if there was a unanimous decision to have me in the company. Tom returned to say there was such agreement. I joined, telling them that once I had a 10 percent shareholding I would change our Southland operation to Mobil fuel. In time that was what happened.

But Mobil was also changing its modus operandi, placing more and more of their business in the hands of distributors. With new distributors they insisted on equity. They had no equity in Gore Services, of course, because it had started operations as an agency, not a distributor. It was a considerable change because the distributor, rather than just carting the fuel and charging Mobil for the mileage, had to buy the fuel. From the moment it was collected at the port, the fuel belonged to the distributor who then had to sell it, carry the book debt and pay Mobil. There was a lot more money involved.

Mobil became nervous and wanted shares in any existing distributorships which Gore Services did not want to do if they could help it. Then Mobil changed its tack. Representatives approached me and asked if I would take up a 50 percent shareholding in the company so they had one major shareholder to deal with. We agreed, and as shareholders sold out we ended up with 50 percent of the company. Other transport operators own the other half. The company developed from there, ably managed by Gary Richardson (no relation) for more than 25 years.

In 1993, 10 years after my first introduction to Mobil, we had another opportunity to expand. Mobil wanted to establish a distributorship based in Christchurch. Gore Services approached the fuel company but was rejected because of a company

Gore Services Ltd was a relatively simple operation, with its tanker and fuel supply business for farmers, and after we joined, we found other new opportunities. As shown on the truck they were also the Foden agents.

When we took over the Southland Carrying Company in 1988, we bought the business that had fond memories for me as a child. They had an immaculate fleet of trucks.

policy not to allow one distributor to start up in another region. I think they were worried they might lose control, particularly to Gore Services in which they had no equity.

But they had no qualms about H W Richardson Group taking up shares in a distributorship in Canterbury. As well we could bring them new volume for fuel through our operations in Canterbury, where we were still using Caltex. Eventually we formed a 50/50 partnership with Mobil called Allied Petroleum. We do the administration and it's been a successful distributorship. Our connection with Mobil has been through some testing times as Mobil rationalised, however. For the first 18 months of the Allied Petroleum partnership we didn't have the same Mobil directors for two meetings in succession.

* * *

On one occasion my interests grew through tragedy. Transport was relatively close-knit and I met and became friends with many people within the industry. One in this category was Fred Andrews, a larger than life character who lived near Riversdale. Fred owned Argyle Station, a huge property of more than 30,000 acres, as well as Andrews Transport, which operated out of Riversdale with about 18 trucks after Fred had taken over from Alf Bishop in Waikaia, merging that business with Stewarts Transport, of Riversdale. Fred was largely a rural carrier so he was not directly in opposition to us.

Fred had started with nothing but had worked his way up from the Mataura freezing works, catching possums and so on to become very well known in the Riversdale area. He had done extremely well and was enormously respected. Then, on 13 April 1984, he had walked behind a truck at a loading bank when the hand brake released. Fred was crushed. His death was a shock.

I was asked to become a director to help the trustees keep the business going and I agreed. My involvement at that level lasted for nine years but a board of directors and trustees were not an ideal way to run a transport company. Eventually, two of the company's long-serving drivers, Peter Stevenson and Murray Maslin, decided to start up their own business. After some discussion with the owners it was decided a better resolution would be to offer the drivers an interest in Andrews. They managed to find enough money to make a bid for half of the company. They made the offer on the basis that the trustees would keep the other half and sell it to them over a period of time. But, at the last minute, the trustees pulled back, saying it was an all or nothing deal.

Keeping the business wasn't really an option and it was offered to two other operators. One turned it down and the other wouldn't meet the price the trustees wanted. So the 50-50 deal with Peter Stevenson and Murray Maslin was resurrected and, to keep the deal alive, I offered to buy the other 50 percent. The deal was done, and has worked successfully ever since. Of course, this put us back into rural transport which I had previously quit.

* * *

In 1988, we bought the Southland Carrying Company, which had been established in the late 1920s, and merged it with Purdues. Southland Carrying Co had had various owners and partners, but Jim McGoldrick, my friend from childhood, was the man associated with it for most of its history. Originally, it was called Withington and McGoldrick, but the company split, with Withingtons going on their own account and McGoldrick teaming up with Watts and Grieve Ltd and others. Watts and Grieve, in a prime inner city site, were the Morris car and truck agents.

Southland Carrying Company was formed into a limited company in 1933, with involvement from Watts and Grieve and later Southland Frozen Meat Ltd. It was one of the earliest companies to cart livestock, an activity that expanded rapidly in the 1940s, and it ended up with a fleet of some 11 Thornycroft trucks, several of them diesel, plus some others. Watts and Grieves had been agents for them but, after the Second World War, the Carrying Co became the agents.

In 1958 Maurice and Russell Carnahan took over the company and, when we took them over, they had an immaculate fleet of trucks. In the meantime they had got out of rural cartage and were involved only in carrying around the city.

Indirectly that purchase also meant we owned Singer Carriers, another well-known Southland company established in the 1930s. Russell Carnahan had bought out Singer and merged it into Southland Carrying Company.

Singer had been owned by Reg Haywood, whom I knew. As a young man, Reg had started his working life milking cows for an old Oteramika Road farmer who used to wake him every morning by bashing on the door of the hut in which he lived.

One Monday morning, the farmer had banged his door and called out: "Get up, you lazy bugger. The day after tomorrow is Wednesday. Half the week gone and nothing done."

Reg decided milking cows wasn't for him and started in transport with a motorcycle and sidecar. He called himself Shilling Carriers but when he put up his

Southland Freight Haulage Ltd came into our hands in 1989 after the demise of Transpac. Among its contracts was carting aluminium to Bluff from the Tiwai Point aluminium smelter.

The long-established Empire Forwarding Company's vehicles were very familiar in Invercargill streets. We bought the company in 1993 and the Bluff Carrying Company, controlled by the legendary oyster boat owner, Stan Jones, not long afterwards.

price from the shilling equivalent of 10c to 15c he had to change his name. By that time, he had a little Singer car converted to a truck, and so Singer Carriers were born, a name he would keep for the rest of his business life.

Another large transport operator fell into our hands in 1989 when we bought the Invercargill branch of Transpac from the receivers of that company. It was the original Southland Freight Haulage Ltd, which had been owned by Ian Guise and others before he sold to Southland Frozen Meat Ltd. When that company got into financial difficulty its board decided to stick to its knitting and sold it to an Australian-owned company which floated it on the Stock Exchange. Those who managed Transpac should have stuck to whatever they did previously as well.

Transpac did not last long, going broke in a big way. We spent a lot of money re-equipping the Transpac fleet which fortunately had the contract for carrying aluminium to the wharf from the aluminium smelter. Russell Carnahan, from whom we had bought Southland Carrying Company, offered to run it for six months to sort it out, and is still with us.

At the same time, Gore Services bought Transpac's Gore branch which originally had been Cunningham Transport. Again, it was mainly rurally based, with some freight. So much for my intention of getting away from rural transport.

In April 1993 we were approached to buy Empire Forwarding Ltd, a long-established and high profile carrying company in Invercargill. It was started in 1925 by S McDonald and Co, shoe proprietors in Invercargill and Gore. Samuel McDonald had owned sample rooms in a building called the Empire buildings. In those days, travellers would send their wares to each town by rail. They were picked up, taken to the sample rooms and the travellers would invite prospective buyers to come and inspect. They took the orders then bundled up their samples and sent them to the next town.

Samuel McDonald saw an opportunity in this and started a business forwarding the samples on, and combined the name of the building with the business to establish Empire Forwarding Co. Then in 1939 he bought out the quite large Pope Bros. Pope's trucks were painted cream and Empire's trucks were green. After 1939 the cream was placed on top of the green and that was the fleet colour of Empire Forwarding until the time we bought it.

Graham McDonald, the third generation, decided to sell when he learned that the Tiwai Point aluminium smelter, to which they had the contract for all inward freight, wanted that contract held by the same company that did all the rest of their work. That company was, of course, Transpac or Freight Haulage, which we had bought in 1989. Graeme was not interested in competing for all the smelter's business and wanted to get out.

We therefore weaved some of Empire Forwarding's business into Freight Haulage, some into Purdues and the rest into Southern Transport.

Another purchase with long links to the past was A1 and City Carriers, although it had just three trucks by the time we bought it from The Southland Times. Originally it had been called the Bob Carriers run by Frank and Sid Maxted, and later F and S Maxted and then S Maxted until The Southland Times bought it.

Sid was called "Night and Day" Sid because he worked night and day. He used to cart our timber from the rail, dropping it in our yard at 7 o'clock at night, before heading for the Longwoods to bring a load of timber from there to Invercargill. But he would be back at the rail early in the morning in time to put on a load of timber by hand and have it in our yard by 8 o'clock in the morning.

1993 turned out to be another very busy year for our transport interests. In October, as we were putting together the Allied Petroleum deal with Mobil, we bought Herberts Transport at Edendale with Jim Dynes, a Tapanui transport operator. Again, after 73 years in family ownership, the third generation wanted out.

We considered it a tidy little business and Edendale was the home of a burgeoning dairy industry in Southland. The glory days of the sheep industry were gone. The Southland meat export industry had shrunk from four major freezing works to three, and meat companies were killing nowhere near the numbers of sheep and lambs they had killed in the past.

As a result many farms had converted from sheep to dairy, with dairy farmers from the North Island and their vast herds of cows heading south to take advantage of relatively stable prices in a growing market and, compared with the North Island, low land prices. We bought Herberts on speculation and were delighted when a lot of work in whey spreading and the likes eventuated from the only dairy factory in Southland at Edendale. An 8-truck business became a 14-truck business in no time at all.

The Bluff Carrying Company, established in 1946 in the port town, was our next acquisition. It had been controlled by Stan Jones, a legendary Southland oyster boat owner, who had died. We bought the company from his estate and wound it into our other businesses.

Next we did a deal to buy a quarry at Greenhills, near Bluff, in equal partnership with Fulton Hogan. It's called Greenhills Quarry Ltd, producing dunite for fertiliser, mostly for SouthFert at Awarua nearby, and some for Ravensdown, the other major fertiliser manufacturer in the South Island. As well, it produces roading material for the general public.

In February 1996, we became involved with Peter MacKay and Robin McCall, of MM Transport, in Gore, and Ian (Inky) Tulloch, son of Mac, who was running his father's business out of Mataura. The Tulloch interests owned Eastern Transport and Ross Transport in Gore, and it was decided to wind them all into one company called Hokonui Haulage Ltd. Gore Services Ltd owns 30 percent, Tullochs 45 and Peter and Robin have the remaining 25 percent.

In August that year my intention to get out of rural transport went further west when we bought out Kapuka Transport, which was based in Kapuka and Tokanui in southern Southland, where Richardsons had had a presence many years before. There was also a lot of trucking history in the company.

Kapuka Transport was made up of various carriers, Gorge Road Transport, Chisholm Bros, of Tokanui, Kapuka Transport and Hollands and Pearman at Ashers Siding which had been together then split apart. Eventually they were all brought together and ended up in Kapuka Transport. I was pleased to take it over for a more personal reason as well.

I had known John Lloyd, who was second in charge of the company, for many years. He had driven for us at one stage, as had his father, Les, who had worked for us for 17 years. John was the second generation in the transport industry and he was keen to advance. A few months before the Kapuka opportunity arose, he had approached me to see if we had any suitable management positions. We didn't at the time. Three months later his boss decided to sell. I decided to buy and let John run it.

The Kapuka Transport purchase added another 12 trucks to the fleet and, late in 1996, we added another 16. We were approached to buy a few shares in Transport Services Ltd in the coal mining town of Nightcaps. It had been the local branch of the ill-fated Transpac and, prior to that, was called S and J McRae Ltd, which operated from the 1930s. Local farmers and existing staff had bought it after the Transpac collapse, and they approached us when two of the shareholders wanted to sell out. We had no sooner become involved when D T King and Co, of Pukemaori, made a bid to take over the company. It was either back off or buy it ourselves. We opted for the latter.

S and J McRae, from the 1940s to the 1960s, were well known as rural carriers. In the 1940s they had an impressive fleet of K and KB series Internationals, which were truly classic American trucks. They also had a REO, a few Commers and Ford V8s. Then, in the 1950s, they switched to Leyland Comets and had a large fleet of them. If you had Leyland Comets in the 1950s you were made.

In 1997, we bought another Southern Southland company in Waikawa Freight. Brett Harvey, the owner, was planning to shift to Invercargill. It was a small operation consisting of a truck, a licence and the business and we shook on the deal on the side of the road in Bond Place, Invercargill. Then I promptly forgot all about it until the day we were due to take over.

I drove to town to give him the cheque.

"I suppose you thought I wasn't coming back," I said.

"I knew you wouldn't be leaving town," he replied.

That was as formal as it got.

Looking at the history of the businesses – seeing where they came from and where they ended up – I find interesting. For example, Rimu Transport had originally been based in Toa which most people knew as Rimu. It had also incorporated the business of Perriam and Moyles from Waituna. Bob McDowell, of Makarewa, had bought out Jack McRae and built up his business from there. Jack was the brother-in-law of Jack Hogan, whom we had bought in 1968, and we had bought both Rimu and McDowells in 1971.

The histories of the companies reflected much more than the owners, however. They told the stories of opportunities taken, of communities and their development, of social, economic, family and business circumstances and of life itself. They also told, of course, of the development of road transport.

* * *

Road transport was well regulated in the early days and carriers presented a united front to look after their interests through the Road Transport Association. From the earliest days I was involved with the association and for some 19 years attended meetings without a break.

I became president of the Southland branch and Graham McDonald and I were also on the national council for a couple of years, which meant numerous trips

A site to gladden the heart of any true truck enthusiast – S and J McRae's lineup of rural vehicles, photographed in the 1950s. Their impressive fleet included truly classic American trucks.

Two Transport Services Ltd vehicles in Western Southland. Did somebody say we were getting out of rural transport?

to the capital. I don't know if we achieved anything but it was reasonably interesting. Meetings were entertaining because, while we were a group of carriers, the reality was that most of us were in opposition to each other and some of that opposition was quite violent. Carriers didn't hesitate to tell each other what they thought.

In the days of transport licensing we used to discuss each month the upcoming agenda with the licensing authority. That meeting was held just before the hearing date when we would discuss what we would oppose and what we would support. There were always differences of opinion on what we should be doing. Many a long evening I have spent at transport meetings but usually they were not without humour because of the very diverse personalities which those meetings brought to the fore.

On one occasion, a carrier accused another of price-cutting.

"You carted the wheat from a client who had been my client and you cut the price," he accused.

"Name your client," the accused carrier responded.

"I'm not naming the client. I'm just saying that's what you did and I'm not very happy about it."

"Name your client," the accused carrier repeated, and continued to repeat until his accuser shot back: "I'm not going to name the client but all I can say is that you can cart her bloody wheat and drink her gin as well." That obviously left neither of them in any doubt as to who the client was.

In May 1996 we did something we had never done before – we sold a business. Harold had wanted to sell Tregenzas a couple of years earlier because it didn't fit in very well with our other businesses. It wasn't in concrete and all our other transport businesses were in Southland. It was a fairly small operation but to make it large enough to be really worthwhile it would have needed more money. And every time we were faced with that choice we decided it was more worthwhile to invest in Southland.

An opportunity to sell had occurred a few years before, but it would have meant relocation of the company to Christchurch and job losses. We didn't want that to happen so we turned the offer down. Then in May 1996 a Timaru accountant approached us. He had a client who wished to buy and this deal ensured that staff would keep their jobs. The waste disposal side of the company was sold to Fulton Hogan and the rest was sold to Gary Rooney, of Waimate.

It's the only business we've sold, and I hated it.

As one of my last gestures I arranged for the company to pay $2000 to each of seven long-time staff, and $1000 each to three who hadn't been there quite so long. Only one of them said thanks. I'm not saying they didn't appreciate it – I heard second hand they did – but it was an interesting study in human nature.

* * *

The most significant acquisition of 1996 resulted in our becoming involved in the road construction business. For many years the Southland County Council, which became the Southland District Council, had had a fleet of trucks and other equipment for roading purposes. Due to local government reforms it had been turned into a local authority trading enterprise about 1991.

Creating what was called a Late required a hands-off policy by the council and I was on the board of the original establishment unit to determine whether a company should be formed. There were five other members and I was the only one who voted against the idea. I didn't believe the district council should be in that line of activity at all. However, SouthRoads was duly established. I offered to resign but the council asked me to stay on to help get the company running, which I did. It was enjoyable, interesting work.

One of the other members of the establishment committee was Trevor Tattersfield, formerly of Invercargill who had shifted to Christchurch and we were fortunate to hire him as manager. Trevor had been working for Bitumix for about 25 years and had been asked to shift to Auckland, which he didn't want to do. With his private enterprise background Trevor soon had SouthRoads humming very differently from a local body operation.

After two years I resigned from the board because of a perceived rather than an actual conflict of interest. For example, if one of my companies had won a

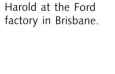
Harold at the Ford factory in Brisbane.

SouthRoads was a major diversification which came about through some interesting negotiations

contract to work for SouthRoads, it would not have been because of my position on the board. But an opposition company which missed out would probably see it that way. I didn't want that sort of hassle so, after the company was up and running, I quit. That turned out to be a fortuitous resignation.

In 1996 I heard through very unofficial channels that SouthRoads was for sale. Had I still been on the board, of course, I would have been prevented from making any offer because that would have been a conflict of interest. Initially, when I approached the district council, I was told it wasn't for sale. But my source was a good one and I persisted, to discover the council had been negotiating to sell to Bitumix.

I went back to the council and asked if I could bid as well and, eventually, I was allowed to, being given a fortnight to get our offer together whereas Bitumix had been allowed several months of due diligence. I didn't feel at too much of a disadvantage, however, because I knew the operation and its people. At the end of 1996 we put in our bid of $10.2 million, a large sum for us, and we were successful.

The purchase of SouthRoads allowed us a major diversification. Mainly Southland based, it had revealed in its short history that it could be innovative. As well, it had a lot of synergies with other companies within the group such as carting gravel and plant hire. It also meant a Southland operation built up by Southland ratepayers stayed in Southland hands and did not slip off to a British-owned company. Whenever I drive around Southland and South Otago I see SouthRoads trucks and equipment and that gives me a lot of personal satisfaction. Road construction isn't an easy business but it's something I feel a real rapport with.

* * *

SouthRoads also helped me work through the immediate repercussions of a personal devastation. Its impact was shattering and its dark cloud will hang over our family for the rest of our lives.

Our son, Harold, was very much a part of the business. He had worked his way through the various operations and one day, it was clear, he would head the company. He had married Julie Wensley and they had built a much-talked-of house in Herbert Street, Invercargill. They had the rest of their lives to look forward to.

Harold hadn't been forced into the business but I would have been very disappointed if he hadn't joined us. He was very like me. He thought like I did and he was perhaps even more ambitious. No matter what he did, he did it well. Sometimes he struggled but he was never slow in learning how to overcome obstacles. Shona and I were so proud of him.

September 27, 1995, is a date burned forever into our memories, Harold and Julie were on a trip around the concrete plants in the North Island. They were driving south of Waiouru when a truck crossed the centre line and collided with their car. Julie received only a slight injury, but Harold was killed. He was 29.

The next day my ailing mother also died. It was the grimmest of times.

Julie and Harold.

HAROLD'S DEATH HAD AN ENORMOUS IMPACT not just on our immediate family but also on staff. He had been working just 13 years but he was part of the company and well liked and respected by those he worked with, even though he was the boss' son. He had earned this respect by himself and, had he lived to take over the company as I had hoped, he too would have been blessed with loyal, devoted people.

All companies owe their staff a great deal. But with us, many seemed almost part of the family. It was something I looked for when we investigated taking over other companies. We looked at the quality of the staff and at the way they regarded their company. The most obvious sign is pride in the company and what it does. A company cannot exist as a name or an entity. A company exists, whether going forwards or backwards, on the quality of the people who work for it. The boss who forgets that ends up owning nothing of real value.

Without the services of our many long-serving staff members we would never have achieved what we have. Their knowledge, experience, advice and loyalty underpins every aspect of our operations. In the end, it's the people who work for the company who determine its culture. Some of the culture must come from the ownership but staff and the attitudes they reflect while on the job and being there determine most of it.

Many of our staff became friends. Frank Crawford ran the mill at Niagara for 38 years, retiring a few years ago. He was with us through all the hard times and knew the strain my father was under. Stu Robertson, who drives for Southern Transport, has been with us 40 years. Likewise, Joe Toma, who died in 1998, retiring the year before due to ill-health, had spent 37 years driving a truck for Southern. Ray Phillips, who runs the company, started with us 30 years ago as a driver.

Les Kennedy was 30 years as a mechanic, Lew Templeton 25 years as a driver and Mick Cordell 26 years as a mechanic and driver at Southern. Joe Bashford worked at Progress Valley for 32 years and there have been others who have given more than 25 years service in companies we have taken over.

Then at Allied, there's Vic Botting, who's been with us 40 years as foreman and manager in Gore and Colin Murray, who has worked with us for a quarter of a century as Invercargill Branch Manager.

These are the sort of people who make the business work. Managers can dream all they like about what they would like to do and how it can be done. But without the right people those dreams will come to nothing.

I often say of truck drivers that there's no difference between an old Bedford and a brand new Mack until you actually sit someone behind the wheel. If you don't have a capable driver they are both useless pieces of machinery. You can only find out the difference between those two pieces of machinery if you have an operator. And without good operators all you have is a lot of used machinery. It also helps when they take a pride in their machinery. That's why, wherever it can be

Lew Templeton has spent more than 25 years with us as a driver at Southern Transport.

done, our drivers have their "own" trucks.

Years ago I made a New Year's resolution that, somewhere throughout the country, I would ride in a truck about once a month. As it turns out, I average more than that. It's a simple process. I stop a truck of any of our companies at any time or any place and ask the driver: "Are you coming back this way?" If the answer is yes, I climb into the cab and do the round with him. I get to talk to the driver, he knows you're taking an interest and you learn a lot from them because they spend a lot of their time thinking about our business because they're part of it.

It's very easy to take for granted the knowledge of our business that they've got in their heads. Without that knowledge none of our companies would start business in the morning. It's too easy to forget that, in our case, if we had to find 360 new operators overnight we wouldn't get on the road. No one would know what to do. So many aspects in the daily running of our business are known only to the people who are doing them every day. If management had to do those jobs, the time and investigation required to find out what does happen, and how to make it happen, doesn't bear thinking about.

Trade unions have existed most of the time we've been in business. We had a very good relationship with the Drivers' Union by and large and had very little industrial trouble. We always tried to treat our drivers fairly and that philosophy went a long way to ensuring we had little difficulty. I had often watched employers treating staff unfairly and it upset me. Again, it reflects that simple fact: we need our people.

When the Employment Contracts Act was introduced in 1991, a union secretary came to me and said: "You employers have it made now because there is unemployment out there and you could replace all your staff tomorrow if you wanted to." I told him he was wrong.

"We need them as much as they need us," I told him. "It's a two-way thing."

Ray Phillips now runs Southern Transport but he started as a union delegate. He was tough but always fair and, when he changed sides and became the manager at Southern, he was the same when representing the other side, which is how it should be.

His three sons drive for the firm. We have seen many such successive generations over the years. I believe that's a sign we can't be too bad. After all, if we treated one generation badly, you can be sure a second wouldn't want to work there as well.

In real estate, it's location, location, location which makes the difference. In business it's people, people, people. Buying equipment and getting good gear are not difficult for any business. But you have to have the right people operating it.

Sometimes you get it wrong. We've chosen the wrong people for a job, and putting them off is never pleasant. And things can go wrong for reasons you can't foresee. For example, you have to have people who can work with other people and a failure in that area can jeopardise an entire operation. Still, having the right people in the right places is an absolute necessity for a successful business.

And people being people, there's always room for humour. On one occasion when I had clambered into a cab in Wellington the driver asked me where I was from.

"Invercargill," I said.

"Invercargill," he mused. "Hmm, I used to live there once."

"Did you really?" I asked in surprise. "Whereabouts?"

"Liffey Street," he laughed.

The penny dropped. Liffey Street was the site of the city's jail. That was in the early days of Capital Concrete and that man, who was heavily tattooed and had obviously seen a lot of life, was extremely proud of how the company had made such an impact in Wellington in a short time.

One Saturday morning in the mid-60s I had dropped into the office which, in those times, wasn't manned. The phone was ringing so I answered it.

"I was the chap who phoned about 10 minutes ago and complained about that driver," the voice at the other end of the line said. "I really don't want him to lose his job so if you just tell him off that will be enough."

I had no idea what he was talking about but humoured him and got off the phone to investigate. It turned out one of our trucks which had been towing a trailer had passed this chap in his old truck and cut in a little quickly. As he did so he took off that truck's side mirror and the driver, naturally upset, had telephoned to complain. The driver of our truck had come straight to the yard and, getting out of his vehicle, heard the phone ringing. On answering it, he listened as a man complained about an incident with one of our trucks, and quickly realised he was the man responsible.

When the man had finished, he told him: "Well, that's not good enough. I'll talk to the driver and fire him immediately."

Unfortunately for our man the chap had had second thoughts about having the driver fired and had rung back. Our driver thought he had got away with it, but he wasn't fired.

Loyal staff are everything to our businesses. With me on one occasion were Joe Pollard, with 18 years service, Joe Toma (37 years) and Colin Murray, manager of our Invercargill Allied plant (25 years).

Some of Southern Transport staff in 1997 – the people who really make it happen.

In Niagara days we had a Miss Muir working in the office. She was really efficient working on the Niagara accounts, which were never in good shape.

One day she said to Jim Farrelly: "Really, Mr Farrelly, this wire rope that you buy just costs an absolute fortune. Is there no way around it?"

Farrelly, dripping with sarcasm, replied: "Well, Madam (as he always called her), next time I'm down at the mill I'll have a yarn to the bushmen and maybe I'll ask them to see if they could knot some flax together and pull the logs with that." Miss Muir got the message that it was difficult to be in the logging business without wire rope.

Miss Muir was not known to back down and that stubbornness once had an impressive result. She had bought a Morris Minor from Watts and Grieve not long after the Second World War. The car leaked. She took it back to the garage time and again where mechanics tried to repair it to no avail. Miss Muir would take it home, put the hose on it, and the car would still be leaking.

This went on for months. Watts and Grieve staff were going crazy and she was far from happy as well. Finally, in desperation, she wrote a personal letter to Lord Nuffield, of Nuffield Scholar fame and chairman of the Nuffield Corporation. Soon afterwards she received a new car. She was not a lady to be put off.

John Gillies, a partner in Webb Stark and Co, worked for us as an accountant and auditor. He was the son of Sir Harold Gillies, a respected plastic surgeon, and John was a very correct Englishman. Almost individually he was responsible for the growth of the sport of squash in New Zealand as he inspired hundreds of would-be players to build courts and take up the sport throughout the country.

Once, when Miss Muir was doing the farm accounts, she asked him: "Tell me, Mr Gillies, what is a wether?"

John Gillies, in his refined English accent, replied: "A wether, Miss Muir, is a male sheep that has been deprived of the ability to perform its natural bodily functions."

This became an often-repeated story around our office for many years.

Even the boss can cause trouble. Once I towed a truck into the yard and parked it. It had broken an axle at the city tip and, as I pulled in with the workshop truck, the driver in the broken-down vehicle let it roll close to the back of the towing vehicle. We got out and he began to work on the broken axle while I went back to the office.

Some time later an emergency arose and I leapt into the workshop truck in great haste, forgetting the two vehicles were still attached. I roared off until I reached the end of the chain when the truck stopped with a great bang and I was fired against the top of the windscreen, hitting my head.

In a confused state, and anxious to be on my way, I tried again. The same thing happened.

The mechanic appeared by my window: "I say, Boss, if you're going to do that a third time, do you think you could let me know in advance so I can climb out from under the truck?"

I had to accept that rebuke from a dry-witted mechanic.

We had another mechanic, very good at his job, but extremely hot-headed. He came into my office one day.

"I'm finishing up," he said.

"Why's that?" I asked.

"Well, I've worked out there's not room in this company for two hot-headed bastards and I can't see you leaving." I didn't want to argue with him. On that note, we agreed to part.

Our driver, Joe Toma, was a master of understatement. One day he telephoned me to say he had hit a post on North Road at the entrance to Invercargill at Waikiwi, and could I come to view the scene.

"Oh, if you've just hit a post, you'll be right," I responded "We'll fix the truck up when you get home. Just carry on."

"No," said Joe, "I'd rather you came out."

I duly went and discovered the post was a very large hardwood telegraph pole which he had hit head on, damaging the front of the truck so severely that it wasn't going to be driven anywhere. Further, the post had broken off and flattened the top of the cab. Joe had all the telephone lines of Western Southland draped around the cab and all over the road.

"What happened?" I asked, as I surveyed the chaos.

"I was bending down to pick up a cigarette I had dropped," he replied.

On the day of Joe's funeral, 36 years later, I learned the accident was not caused by a dropped cigarette at all. Joe was terrified of earwigs and, just before the accident, an earwig had crawled up his windscreen.

On another occasion, about 1965, he telephoned me about 10.30 one night to say he had run off the road.

"Are you OK?" I asked.

"Yes."

A lineup of some of the companies' vehicles at Bluff.

Building the viaduct through the infamous Otira Gorge was a particular challenge for Williams Allied. It was so cold we had to use warm water in the concrete.

"Is the truck damaged?"

"Not really," Joe replied. "It's stuck. If we get it back on the road, we could drive it home."

Joe revealed again that he wasn't prone to exaggeration. It took two wrecking cranes to get it home and we had to get a new chassis from Australia. It was, in fact, bent like a horseshoe and off the road for six months.

Joe also proved a great mimic. Once, in the early days, I had given him a good dressing down for something he had done. When I had finished I told him to get out of my office because I was really wound up. A few minutes later I walked into the main office to find Joe giving other staff a very good impersonation of my telling off. He had it word perfect, complete with actions. I could only laugh. He disappeared, and kept driving.

A character who laid bricks for the firm for many years was Chou Murdoch, known to one and all as Chou. One of a large family of bricklayers, a character who would became a legend in the building industry, he never expected to be called anything else.

We also had a man working for us with a patch over one eye, and Chou did not like him. One day, the man with the patch walked through the yard.

"G'day, Chou," he said.

"G'day, Lord Nelson," Chou replied.

The man stopped. "Don't you ever call me Lord Nelson," he threatened.

"For the record, my name is Walter," Chou replied.

One day in the office at morning tea time Chou was listening to an accountant telling us all in great detail about a huge fish he had caught.

When he had finished, Chou started.

"I went floundering last night at Oreti Beach with my boy and we had a great haul," he said. "It was pretty dark and we just had the dinghy and a Tilley lamp sitting at the end. When we hit a wave it fell into the sea. So I got my boy to jump in and get it. He brought it up and the lamp was still burning."

"That can't be right, the lamp still burning?" the accountant said.

"Yes, it was," said Chou.

"I don't believe that, Chou," the accountant went on. "You couldn't drop a Tilley lamp in the sea and bring it up with the lamp still burning."

Chou looked at him and said: "Okay, I'll do a deal with you."

"What do you mean?"

"You cut that fish in half and I'll blow the lamp out."

A White Russian worked for us. He was hopeless and, after he drove a truck down Dee Street, Invercargill's main thoroughfare, with the handbrake on and the brakes on fire, I went to tell him his days with us were over.

"You misrepresented the job," he responded.

"How do you work that out?" I asked.

"Well, you put an ad in the paper for a truck driver."

"That's right."

"But I am loading the truck and I am unloading the truck. Where I come from, someone else does that so you have misrepresented the job."

I assured him that was the way we did things in New Zealand and, as far as I was concerned, he was down the road. He replied that if I fired him I would have to live with that on my conscience for the rest of my life. I told him I would not have difficulty with that and away he went.

Over the years there have been many characters, including "Silent George," so called because he rarely spoke to anyone. Another of his faults was that he was not good at directions, which is quite important for truck drivers.

In earlier days truck-to-truck and truck-to-base communication was via radio telephones and George taught me a good lesson. One night we were carting grain off headers during the harvest season and I told him I would meet him at the Roslyn Bush School at midnight. I arrived and waited, and waited, and waited. Finally, I called him on the RT and asked him where he was. He was sitting, waiting for me, at the Myross Bush School. I told him what I thought over the RT, which I didn't normally do because the channels were open to all sorts of other people.

Bob McDowell, whom we had not long before bought out, had an RT under his bed so he could keep in touch with his trucks. Bob and his wife heard what I said loud and clear.

"I thought you said Bill Richardson didn't swear," his wife said to him.

"No," said Bob, "I said he didn't drink."

* * *

Lindsay Blackler was a farm manager at Rocklands, an excellent one who had been with us some years. He and his father were particularly close and our connection with the pair was enhanced by the fact that Mr Blackler Senior drove a truck for us at Southern Transport. Most weekends he was at the farm, helping Lindsay. One day in February 1980, Lindsay was carting hay when the tractor rolled and he was killed. It was up to me to tell his father the news that would break his heart.

* * *

We did a lot of difficult work, including house removals, for many years. One of those jobs was shifting the Kapuka School. Les Lloyd, who drove for us for 17 years, was in charge of that shift. Four jacks along each side would be enough to do the job, I assured him.

They started work, then Les called the office.

"This thing's heavy. We need more jacks."

"It can't be that heavy," I said.

"Yeah, it's really heavy."

So I sent down another man and more jacks. The team placed five along each side. Soon afterwards there was another call back to the office.

"We need more jacks. We can't lift it with five jacks."

"What the hell is wrong?" I asked. "We shifted the Merivale School a couple of weeks ago. It was the same size and we didn't need more than four jacks along each side for that."

"Well, it may have been the same size but it wasn't as heavy as this is," the message came back from the team.

"There's something wrong," I said. "I'll come down."

I drove down, checked what they had done and confirmed it wouldn't budge.

"We'll have to get more jacks," I said, helpfully.

"That's what we've been telling you."

Eventually we lifted the school, put it on our trailer and watched it just about bend in half. That meant lifting the school again, extricating our trailer and borrowing an even bigger one from Southland Freight Haulage.

Later that afternoon, I went to Invercargill Airport to pick up my parents who were returning from an overseas trip. As ever, Dad asked me what we had been doing and what had been going on in his absence.

"We're shifting the Kapuka School today," I said.

"I bet that's heavy," he said.

Dad, I knew, had built the school but the reason for our difficulties became obvious when he described how it was built with 6 x 2 red pine studs and inch sarking.

"I wish you'd been here a couple of days ago," I muttered. "You'd have saved me a bit of embarrassment."

Eventually, we stopped moving buildings, even though we did many in the 60s and 70s. It required more specialised equipment and I felt our future lay in other areas.

The world has changed in the meantime, of course, and today people are not so interested in sticking long at jobs. Long-serving veterans are likely to become a thing of the past. The likes of Cyril Kettle, who worked for 50 years at Southland Concrete Products, will disappear. That business actually was Cyril. He worked there, although he had had a few shares in the early days of the company, and he treated it as his own.

It wasn't a great working environment, archaic in some ways, which could lead to health problems later, and hard work. With automation, fork lifts and so on, the work became easier, as needed to happen. But you still need people to do such work and it will become harder and harder to find them. In such workplaces treating people fairly is paramount.

John Neiborg, who manages Concrete Products, began there before we took over ownership 19 years ago and his experience is invaluable. Employers need people who stick at their jobs.

Overall we employ 550 people. Large firms like ours tend to become impersonal. I try to avoid that but obviously our company is not as personal as it was when we had 100 staff. That means I have to try harder, getting around our people as much as possible. That's a big ask, particularly with our North Island branches, so it's something I emphasise to our regional managers – treat these people as you would want to be treated yourself.

Yet we've found it's not hard to pass around a culture that encourages staff loyalty and makes them feel part of the group. When we took over

Kapuka School certainly took some shifting.

Cyril Kettle worked for Southland Concrete Products for 50 years. This photo was taken when he was over 80 years of age.

Rimu Transport, Charlie Jack had been driving there for 11 years or so.

"Are you coming with us?" I asked him.

"Oh, I don't know how I'd get on working for a big firm," Charlie replied. We were hardly huge in those days but Southern Transport had about 30 staff while he was used to the six at Rimu.

"Well, will you give it a go?" I asked. Charlie said he would and he retired 19 years later. The perception was worse than the reality. Once again it's a matter of how people are treated and if they are treated decently they will slot into a bigger operation no trouble at all.

We also produce a newsletter called Allied Views for staff around the country to try to let people in different areas know what we are doing in other places. If we don't do that they have no idea of the overall picture. For instance, people in Auckland have little idea what the business does in Southland, and vice versa, but most of the staff are interested in what we do. They are interested in trucks and equipment, so we try to feature those items, and the feedback we get is that it creates a lot of interest. Hopefully, it also gives them a feeling of belonging to a larger organisation and not feeling they are just a number.

Even though we have many different companies, because of our different ownership structures and locations, we hope they can still identify with the business they are working for under the larger umbrella of H W Richardson Group. We strive to achieve the best of both worlds.

Of course there are times when you are let down by staff, even by those you have helped. Mark Twain wrote that if you take a starving dog and feed it, it will not bite you, and that's the fundamental difference between dog and man. That's a fairly cynical view but on occasions there's a grain of truth in it. But you can't let bad experiences stop you helping somebody else. When it happens you have to turn the other cheek and say: "Well, that's that. It didn't work."

It's happened to us on a few occasions when we helped people in business through partnerships and so on and later found we were taken advantage of. But there's no point in grieving over such matters.

It's my belief that the people who work for us are basically good, want to get on with their lives and bring up their kids and do all the normal things that people want to do and achieve. Unfortunately the publicity goes to the no-hopers and those who bleat about their circumstances. I've found that most of our people don't think those sort of negative images at all. They want to provide for their families and are prepared to work to do it. As long as that continues I think everyone has a future in this country.

The same principle, therefore, must also apply to our suppliers. If you don't allow them to make a reasonable profit they won't be there when you need them. It doesn't matter whether they are oil companies, franchise holders, tyre supply people or whatever, they have to make a profit, just as we have to do likewise. Too many people tend to try to screw their suppliers to the last drop of blood and, while times are hard, you have to drive hard deals. But you also have to be fair and that's how we expect to be treated in return.

For example if we have a problem with a truck, we expect the supplier to say: "Yes, that's a truck problem and we'll cover it under warranty." If it's not, we expect them to say: "Well, you did that." Then they should give us a reason why it was our fault and, if the reasoning is sound, we'll accept it. There's no point in driving people to the wall for the sake of a few extra short-term dollars.

We would like to think our customers think the same way. In many instances, they do; in some, they don't. And that's a matter for us. We can choose to work with them, or we can walk away, as we have done.

But there's a particular satisfaction in dealing with long-time customers, such as SouthFert (formerly the Southland Co-operative Phosphate Company), or Craigpine Timber, of Winton. We have six to seven trucks working for that company full time, carrying logs and chips. Over the years, we have also done a lot of work for Stresscrete, carting bridge beams, concrete panels and those sorts of things. That relationship began in 1965.

You also need to support local people, such as engineering companies. If we don't support them, particularly in Southland and smaller-populated cities and districts, there won't be any local people to do the work. When you combine local support with local purchasing, companies have an influence on what happens in a local area. If you don't support local industry whenever possible you're not doing the local economy too many favours.

The hard part, of course, is being personally involved as the boss. If I was heading a corporate in Auckland, life would be easy making such decisions. I'd probably be swapping jobs every three or four years, mouthing on about having moved the company into new strategic directions and that, having succeeded in that task – whatever it was – I'm now seeking fresh challenges. Then I'd jump out on a golden parachute. That's easy because, in the end, there's no responsibility, let alone accountability.

If one of our businesses has attracted attention in some way it tends to be Bill Richardson who's done it. I'm identifiable, people know me. But the advantages far outweigh the disadvantages and I wouldn't have it any other way.

* * *

I'd have to say I like doing deals and one of our best occurred in April 1998. It came our way because the people we were dealing with appreciated that we had kept our word.

It had its beginnings in 1990 when a Tauranga contractor, Albert Smith, contacted Harold, who was then living in Christchurch. Albert had won the contract to build a container wharf at Port Chalmers, near Dunedin. I knew the people of Palmers, the only readymix supplier in Dunedin, well. It was headed by a man called Jim Palmer and their major interest was a long-established quarry in the city. I was prepared to stay out of Dunedin as long as other companies did. Fletchers, I understood, had agreed to a similar arrangement as long before as 1946.

Albert Smith asked his father, John, to manage the Port Chalmers project and found he would have to deal with Palmers for his readymix. But before work started John Smith and Jim Palmer had a major falling out. Albert Smith contacted Harold to ask him to price the job. Knowing my feelings about Palmers, Harold contacted me.

Trucks line up for their loads of phosphate at Bluff. Our relationship with SouthFert, formerly Southland Co-operative Phosphate Company, has been long and good.

"We've already told him we don't want to go into Dunedin against Palmers," I said.

"Well, we do a lot of concrete for Albert," Harold replied. At the time we were providing the readymix for the Tauranga wharf which Albert was also constructing. "We don't want to be too off-hand."

I considered that and then told him: "Tell Albert we'll price the job but ring me before you do so."

Soon afterwards, Harold rang back and said: "We got the job."

"I told you not to price it," I said.

"I didn't price it," Harold replied. "As soon as I said we would price it, Albert said 'The job's yours. I'll send down the papers.' "

It was a Friday. I thought to myself, we have a bit of a problem. I decided to think about it over the weekend and do something the following Monday.

Fortunately Jim Hunter, one of the principals at Palmers, realised there was a communication problem between the Smiths and Jim Palmer and he decided to call on John Smith.

"You're too late to talk about the concrete," Smith told him. "We have given the job to Allied, and they haven't even priced it."

It was fortunate he added the last phrase because it confirmed what I was to tell Palmers. I also said we would put our plant on the wharf at Port Chalmers and not sell concrete to anybody else, thereby not getting into their market.

Fletchers, of course, got to hear of this, and spoke to Palmers. In their minds, the deal meant we were in Dunedin and that allowed them to forget about past agreements as well. Unless Palmers would sell out to them, or sell them Shiel Concrete, another company owned by Palmers, they would start a new plant. Palmers told them to go ahead and they began converting an old Winstones block plant.

Our deal did not upset Palmers and our friendship remained. I was speaking to Jim Hunter one day as the job was finishing at Port Chalmers.

"Pity about Fletchers," I said. "I always wanted to be in Dunedin but now they're going to be here and we're not."

"Well," said Jim, "we'll sell you Shiels. If we're going to have Fletchers as opposition, we won't need all our plants."

Palmers, in fact, had four plants – two at Logan Point, an old one and a new one, one at Mosgiel and the Shiel plant in Glen Road, near the famous sports ground, Carisbrook.

"If you want to come in we'll sell you Shiel Concrete." It was a significant concession because we would be in direct competition with them as well as Firth.

We bought it and started operations immediately, and therefore before Firth.

Jim Palmer, the company's head, eventually died and in the fullness of time Palmers decided that quarrying was their real business and wanted out of readymix. Jim Palmer had run that side of the business and nobody else was enthusiastic.

Out of the blue one day in April 1998 Jim Hunter arrived at my office and asked if we wanted to buy them out. I said we did and soon after the deal was done. We then closed the old Shiel plant and now operate from Logan Point and Mosgiel, but mainly at the former. We had started out in Dunedin as a reluctant participant and ended up a major player.

Earlier we had been involved with John Smith in another deal which resulted in our buying Rangiora Concrete. John owned that company but, at the time, was away in Northland building a bridge. It was the only deal I've ever done where I didn't meet the person I was dealing with for the entire period of the negotiation.

Later, I said to John: "The only thing I missed about that deal was when I agreed to the price which I thought was plenty, I didn't get to see the smile on your face."

If memory serves me correctly all the trucks broke down the first day we operated at Rangiora.

Our geographical spread had also been advancing. In 1997, Allied Milburn bought Ready Mix Concrete Ltd's Taranaki operations from Milburn and, changing the name to Allied, began working in Hawera, New Plymouth, Stratford and Waitara. Allied Milburn also bought O'Hara's in Wanganui the same year, as well as a plant in Tairua, in the Coromandel.

The fastest readymix purchase I made occurred in 1998. Makikihi is a tiny town about 30km south of Timaru. One Saturday morning my nephew, Ross, and I were driving south in a new eight-wheeler MH Mack we had gone to Wellington to collect.

We were approaching Makikihi when a Falcon ute passed us.

"That chap's waving us down," Ross said.

At nearby Otaio Community Hall the ute pulled in and I pulled in as well. Ross and I got out of the truck and I recognised the ute driver as Les Fowler, one of the owners of Makikihi Transport. We had always had a good relationship with them, and they had helped us out with concrete trucks over the years in Timaru. Ross disappeared and Les and I greeted each other.

"I'm pleased I saw you," Les said. "Do you want to buy our readymix operation?"

"Oh, yes, I suppose we would," I said.

"Okay, we'll get it valued," Les continued. "There are only two trucks and one of them we bought from you a while ago."

"Well, that'll be a good truck then," I said.

"It is now," Les grinned. "The other one we bought new, so we'll get the plant valued and that'll be that."

We shook hands on the deal. At that moment Ross re-appeared and I introduced them.

"I just sold your uncle our readymix business," Les said.

"Hell," said Ross, "I only went round the back of the hall to have a leak. I come back and he's bought another readymix business."

12

PEOPLE MAKE OUR BUSINESS GO ROUND but they in turn rely on the tools we give them to do the job. Over the years we have bought some excellent pieces of machinery which have allowed our business to go forward and flourish. We have also purchased others that would have tested the patience of a saint.

The years have passed but I can still remember many of the details. For example, when we took over Niagara Sawmilling, Southern Transport and Richardson had two three-axle, nine ton Ford Thornton trucks as well as a 1949 Ford two-axle five-tonner and a 1951 Bedford Model M three-tonner. Niagara had about 12 steam engines, including the 14 and 20 horsepower Marshall portable steam engines we installed at the Mokoreta mill. At Blackhorn there were two identical Marshalls while Progress Valley mill had a 27hp Garrett stationary steam engine that has since been preserved. There was also a Fowler traction engine at Progress Valley for dragging logs off rail tractors while three of our six log haulers in the bush were powered by Marshall steam engines, two by Johnstons and one by a Burrell.

Then there was our Cletrac DDH bulldozer, with a Heil blade and Carco winch, bought in 1950. It's easily recalled. I still have the original brochure complete with price. Our four 12-wheel-drive rail tractors were locally built – one powered with a GM 3-71 engine and another with a Blackstone Diesel were built by Wilson Bros in Invercargill, and two were built by H E Melhop Ltd. One was powered by a Leyland 450 cubic inch diesel and the other by a four-cylinder White petrol truck engine.

Purdue Bros and their crane trucks and their possible uses show how technology keeps improving.

Allied Concrete's plant at Manukau, Auckland.

That was just the beginning of a life-long purchasing programme. In 1955, we bought a new HD5 Allis Chalmers bulldozer with a Hewco blade and a Carco winch and a K55 Hanomag crawler with a blade made by Johnstons in Invercargill and a Hanomag winch. The latter proved to be useless. It probably wasn't a bad tractor but it wasn't suitable for our line of work. Apart from a Ford truck in 1974, which just wouldn't go properly, that was the only machine we have sent back. We replaced the Hanomag with a second hand Caterpillar D6 9U with a Hyster winch for the bush.

Our purchase of Niagara had coincided with the realisation that steam was a means of producing energy that belonged to the past so we launched into a programme of moving to diesel-powered generation. Dad went to a sale at Lindsay and Dixon's box factory at Drummond in 1956 and bought a 5L3 Gardner diesel which we used to re-power the Mokoreta mill and a 6-71 GM which made the Blackhorn mill more efficient. From another sawmill at Groveburn he bought a Leyland 600 cubic inch industrial power unit which drove the Progress Valley mill.

A second hand rail tractor 3-71 GM engine was used to re-power a steam hauler while a 5LW Gardner engine from an Allen trenching machine re-powered another. A third steam hauler found a new lease of life when we took the 450 cubic inch Leyland off the rail tractor and put it on the hauler. Three diesel-powered haulers and sawmills simplified our operations, although it wasn't easy. We didn't have any money and everything but the HD5 bulldozer was second hand.

When we bulldozed roads into the bush at Progress Valley, we bought a reconditioned GMC 6 x 6 log truck with a GMC

Jinker trailer from Gillies in Oamaru. It was a good machine and we were to buy three of them. Then in 1957 we replaced the Thorntons with that year's Commer diesel and a Thames Trader 75 diesel the following year, while the old Cletrac was replaced with a new Allis Chalmers HD6 in 1959.

At the farm we had started with a David Brown Cropmaster. A David Brown Trackmaster crawler with a blade for pushing gorse followed. It was not a good machine mechanically and we did a deal with the agents to replace it with a slightly later and slightly better tractor called a 30T. It wasn't terrific either but our next purchase, a 50TD David Brown crawler, turned out to be excellent and one of the best crawlers we owned.

Then there was a Hanomag R27, an 850 David Brown, two David Brown 900 diesels, one new, one second-hand, and a new David Brown 990. We also had a 640 DT Fiat, 780 DT Fiat, a 1000 DT Fiat, a 980 DT Fiat, all of which were four-wheel-drive, and a 780 Fiat which actually broke in half, much to the embarrassment of its agents, Andrews and Beavan. In the following years we bought a 634 International 4 x 4 and a 574 International 4 x 4. One of the last tractors was a John Deere four-wheel-drive 3140. We also had an Allis Chalmers roto baler.

One of the more cussed pieces of equipment man ever made were the early chainsaws. We had some seven two-man Titan Bluestreak chainsaws for the bush as well as three Disston Mercury chainsaws. They were unreliable, heavy and prone to being damaged when trees dropped on them or when dozers backed over them, sometimes by accident and sometimes deliberately. In pieces they would be returned to the mill in an apple box. This happened so often that the insurance company refused to cover them, much to the disgust of Dad and Jim Farrelly.

International bulldozers were a favourite at Niagara. We bought two TD15Bs second hand, then two new TD15Cs, which did a lot of work for us. They were not trouble free but they did the job. The last dozer we bought was a Caterpillar D6D, which was a very good machine.

When we started general carrying in the 1960s, and through the early 1970s, our pattern was to buy mainly Commer and International trucks. Then the purchase of second hand Mercedes trucks showed the wisdom of getting out of petrol-driven

The forests at Taringatura, Central Southland, ring to the sounds of Southern Transport trucks and trailers.

One thing I like to do is get into one of our trucks and talk to the drivers. Coming or going, they are a great source of knowledge about our business.

trucks while the purchase of our first Mack truck in 1974 would lead to a long association with the brand. By the mid-1980s we were well into readymix concrete and, when we bought out the various companies, we would usually find their trucks were worn out. The first new trucks we bought were British Dodges with V8 Perkins engines. With dozers, cranes, tractors and trucks, we did a lot of business with International Harvester Company and the local dealers.

There is no doubt in my mind that what happens in childhood has a very strong influence in later life. My grandfather's purchase of his International and Diamond T trucks began a family preference for American vehicles. The Diamond T was commandeered during the war. When he and Dad went to Burnham Military Camp at the end of the war to find it, it had been sold. Grandad bought a second-hand, three-ton, 1937 Ford V8 instead.

Shortly after that, Dad sold his first car, a 1938 Hillman, and bought a 1947 Mercury, a fairly new car and a very up-market, de luxe model. After that he stayed with Canadian Ford cars and bought three such trucks as well. Undoubtedly that influenced me. You often hear of brand loyalty but many people are influenced by what happens in their early years and they hold on to such influences. Farmers and their tractors are the same. Brand preferences pass from generation to generation.

American Ford trucks were not available in New Zealand for many years but, once they came back on the market in 1991, we started buying American Ford trucks for our concrete operations and a few other jobs.

I was probably an easy target. I knew about the Louisville model which had been introduced in the United States in 1972 and, when it was eventually available in New Zealand, we were obvious prospective customers. Harold dealt with the Ford representative on his first visit and listened to his patter.

"Well," he said, "you've got two things going for you. Dad likes American trucks and he likes Fords." We decided to buy two to see what they were like and, when they turned out well, ideally suited as light tare weight concrete trucks, we kept buying them. Now, with 90 such vehicles, we are the largest fleet owner of American Ford Louisville trucks in New Zealand, which have become Sterlings after Daimler Chrysler bought Ford's Louisville truck business.

With such long-standing purchasing relationships we naturally developed relationships with the people who worked for the various companies. At International Harvester, two of the more notable were Nigel Ower and Geoffrey Johnston, who were always ready for all sorts of deals.

In 1975 I was trying to trade in a log skidder for a truck and we couldn't agree on the last $500 on the trade-in price.

"I'll toss you for it," Nigel Ower said.

I refused because I figured if he was ready to lose it on a toss of a coin he was ready to give in anyway. So after months and months of trying I finally sold the Clark 555 skidder which was in good condition but which we simply didn't need any more. The next day gale-force winds struck Canterbury, bringing down trees and entire plantations, and suddenly log skidders were in short supply.

We had a reasonable run with log skidders. We had started with a Timberjack 205 diesel then bought the Clark 555. A second-hand Timberjack 404 was next, followed by a new Tree Farmer C7 with a 4-53 diesel engine. Then the New Zealand Forest Service changed the rules and sawmillers could no longer do their own logging and we didn't need them any more.

The change from petrol-driven to diesel-driven trucks was a huge move. The petrol engines in the Internationals wore out unbelievably quickly in some models, and with such difficulties those personal relationships become important.

At one stage International Harvester sent out a bulletin recommending a certain grade of oil. We bought our oil from Caltex, whose representative advised the recommended oil wasn't the one to use and strongly advised against it. However, I felt that if International, which built the trucks, was recommending a particular oil I should follow their advice. It turned out to be bad advice. Motors wore out even more quickly.

"You're right," I told the Caltex man. "That oil's no good."

"There's nothing wrong with that oil," he replied.

I was puzzled. The Caltex man had been proved right.

"But you told us not to change and we did change on International's recommendation."

"There's nothing wrong with our oil," he repeated.

I could see he was frightened we would claim on them. I assured him we wouldn't because he had told us not to use it. At the same time he was not prepared to admit that the recommended type of oil was the wrong one for the job. It was a typical "nothing is wrong with our product" attitude even when he had recommended us not to use it.

Still, there was a reasonable outcome from our viewpoint. Ian Muggeridge was service manager and handled claims for International Harvester. He came to Invercargill and inspected one of our worn-out motors. Climbing into the truck he had a look about and asked what sort of oil we were using. I told him.

"Who told you to use that stuff?" he asked. I told him.

He climbed out of the truck and asked: "How many motors do you want?"

They paid up for four and no further questions were asked.

We did have one run-in with them, however, which went all the way to their headquarters in Chicago. We had leased International Harvester a building in Otepuni Avenue for their construction equipment, which they sold locally themselves

The Southern Transport fleet and the effect of the business it has generated cannot be under-estimated in the history of our company.

rather than through dealers. The company wanted a large slab of concrete in front which we were prepared to do as long as they paid for it.

We duly poured the concrete but we didn't get paid because the appropriate permission from Chicago hadn't been given. It was quite a large sum so we continued to send the bill. We argued we had delivered our part of the deal and they should honour theirs. After about a year of constant argument we were holding some money we owed them as contra.

Then a new financial controller arrived from offshore, as these multi-national companies which like to transfer people are inclined to do, and he wrote a very curt letter. He could find no record of any money owed so why were we sending this account to them. He wanted our comments by return mail.

Of course there was no record apart from the bill because the local people didn't have the appropriate permission from Chicago. I showed the local representative the letter. He was embarrassed by what had happened and advised me to reply.

"You don't have to say much," he said. "Just write back and make a comment like he asked you to."

I followed his advice with a very simple letter.

"Dear Sir," I wrote, "You must be a new bastard," and signed it.

It produced the reaction I was looking for. Shortly thereafter we were paid.

If we add up the number of heavy trucks we have bought over the years, Fords are dominant. We have also bought 21 N Series Fords which were Japanese Hinos badged as Fords. Altogether we have bought 113 new, heavy duty Ford trucks in the years we have been in business.

Mack is next with 93 and International follows with 72. We have also bought 28 new Nissans, 30 Hinos, 19 Mercedes, 20 Volvos, 11 Commer/Dodges, six Leylands, five Kenworths, three Renaults, three Freightliners, seven Fodens, one Scania, three MAN and one IVECO Cargo.

Thus we have bought a total of 422 new trucks. Through takeovers and acquisitions we have inherited far more than that, not counting lighter vehicles such as pick-ups and utes of which we have had too many to count. Our total number of trucks owned over the years is well in excess of 1000.

The most vital lesson to be learned from buying equipment is simple: buy the right gear for the conditions and the tasks at hand. That takes experience and knowledge. What has advantages in one area may have disadvantages in another that will make the purchase unwise. It also keeps staff happier because they know or soon find out when the boss is taking short cuts.

* * *

All pieces of machinery have their interesting characteristics, their good points and their faults. Over the years designs and technologies have changed; those changes reflect better knowledge of what makes machinery more efficient and powerful. But that doesn't render machinery whose time has past any less valuable in my view. They've done what they were designed to do and, if a business has chosen wisely, done it well. Those pieces of machinery also reflect history and memories.

My passion for machines meant I was often loathe to part with some of the more memorable. I may have bought and owned hundreds of trucks but most of them were more than just another truck in the Richardson fleet. On occasions Harold and I had agreed we had bought a truck more with our hearts than with our heads.

Therefore it was perhaps inevitable I would take up truck collecting as a hobby. In 1967 I had an urge to try to find an old International truck my grandfather had owned. It was a 1933 International Model D1 and he had brought it to Invercargill when moving his business into the city in 1935. I found it only two blocks from home and paid £5 for it.

Over the Christmas period that year, we had gone on holiday to Christchurch where Shona spotted an identical truck in a side street. It was having a new set of spark plugs fitted at a small garage so I waited for the owner to return. When he did I

Grandad's original truck arrives home. It hasn't been restored but I still have it, and a fully restored identical model in better condition.

A Dodge petrol tanker in the museum.

approached him and said I had an identical model at home and wanted one for spares.

"Well, if you give me £85, you can have this one," the owner, who was obviously having some trouble adjusting to decimal currency, said.

I paid him $170 and drove it home from Christchurch with 17-month-old Harold sitting beside me. I never did do up Grandad's truck, although I still have it. Instead I gave the Christchurch one a coat of paint, which was all it needed, and put his name on it. It turned out to have the next consecutive engine number to Grandad's.

For nine years I bought no other old trucks but I knew that the six-wheel International 1938 Model DS216T once owned by Dad was still in Invercargill, having been owned by about four different contractors. By 1976, it was lying in a paddock on the outskirts of Invercargill. Driving past one day I saw sparks coming from it so I stopped. Its owner was about to cut it up for a trailer.

"What have I got to do to stop that happening?" I asked him, explaining it was one of the original trucks we had started Southern Transport with.

"Find me something else to make a trailer out of," he replied.

That presented no difficulty and we dragged the old truck home. It was the first we restored, and International Harvester put it on their trade display at the 1977 transport conference in Invercargill.

A couple of days after the conference, George Wallis, of Wanaka, contacted me. He had seen the International there.

"I see you have a nice International," George said. "Would you like a 1939 Diamond T to go with it?"

As Grandad had had a Diamond T, I was interested, and Harold, then aged about 11, and I drove through snow across the Haast Pass to check it out at the local garage. We looked at it and it joined the collection. Then Ken spotted another one on the side of the road near Oamaru and suddenly my childhood hobby of collecting truck brochures had become an adult one of collecting trucks themselves.

In 1995 my grandfather's original Diamond T, which had been commandeered by the army in 1942, was given back to me by my good friend, Alan Storer, of

Above: Restored to their former glory, trucks stand proudly in part of my truck museum, which attracts more than 2000 people a year from around the world.

Christchurch, who had owned it for 12 years. Alan has been one of the most enthusiastic supporters of my collection, and has provided many interesting items and given freely of his immense knowledge.

    The hobby grew relatively slowly, until I needed a shed to keep them in. Then came more trucks, including the 1936 International C40F, the other truck Southern Transport started business with, along with more sheds until today I have about 150 vehicles and 60,000 square feet of storage space right next door to my home. In 1999 I was invited to address the annual convention of the American Truck Historical Society in Minnesota.

    It's not just the trucks that interest me. There's the actual collection, finding the vehicles, bringing them to Invercargill and restoring them so that they reflect how their makers originally intended them. Then there's the people you meet while doing that. The museum is not directly open to the public as such but close to 2000 people from all over the world visit it every year to look at the various models of trucks and other gear I have collected and, if necessary, restored. That includes old petrol pumps, signs, engines and equipment like truck jacks and so on.

    Groups and individuals alike, I enjoy showing them through. I've got to know so many people, most of whom are not in the transport industry, and have corresponded with or met some of them later overseas. It's become a great hobby. It gets me away from the business and I can lose myself in their restoration through working on them myself.

    It's also been a godsend since Harold's death. Without it I would have found it more difficult to cope.

    New Zealand is a great place to collect trucks because of our climate and because New Zealanders have bought trucks from different countries. In collections in the United States, all the trucks are American and, likewise, in England they are all British. In New Zealand, we have a large selection of both British and American and European, Japanese and others as well.

    I'm becoming more choosy, but the collection will undoubtedly continue to grow. I hope that when I die someone will be interested enough to carry it on.

Epilogue

MANY YEARS AGO I spent an hour with C M Richwhite, the Auckland businessman who had extensive concrete interests, amongst other things. He gave me some good advice. He was highly successful and, apart from readymix operations in Auckland and the Waikato, he ran a company called David Lloyd Ltd, then probably the country's biggest coal merchant after State Coal.

He was 92 and still going to work most days. He told me of his business life – he originally came from the Central Southland town of Winton – as he smoked a cigar in his lower Queen Street office.

As I was about to leave, he said: "I've made a lot of money, young man, but there is one thing you always want to remember. At the end of the day money is no good to you and will not give you any enjoyment unless you have the respect of the people you dealt with while you were making it."

Subsequently I've found that to be true indeed. I have seen people with no money and I've seen people who have made a lot of money. But if you sacrifice the principles of fair dealings, family or a balanced lifestyle to build or run a business and make money you have it the wrong way round, and eventually what you are doing becomes pointless.

I've no doubt that I could have built a bigger business had I sacrificed those or other principles, but what would have been the point. We have an obligation in life to act decently and fairly, particularly towards others, and if you're successful there's far more reward in helping somebody else when such an opportunity comes along. If everybody did that the world would be a better place.

The premature and shocking death of Harold has underlined that belief.

Both Shona and I could say at Harold's funeral service that we had no regrets in our relationship with our only son. Had I been granted an extra 10 minutes with him, knowing that he was going to die, there's nothing I would have said that I hadn't already said. I would have hated to have been in the position where that was not the case.

When we gave that message at the funeral service I was surprised at the number of people who spoke to me privately later, or who wrote to me, saying they had taken what I had said to heart. They suddenly realised, when they saw me standing there with my son dead, that it's too late after the event. I hope they have remembered it.

If you have a problem in a relationship you should fix it while you can. If you fail there's nothing you can do about it. But at least you've tried.

Yet both Shona and I felt something positive had to come from Harold's death. Road fatalities are far more than grim statistics. They haunt families and loved ones for the rest of their lives, and there are always reminders of lives lost suddenly, full potential unrealised. In April 1999 we went to the University of Otago and, with the help of the Land Transport Safety Authority and the university, established the Harold Richardson Memorial Road Safety Students Research Grant of up to $10,000 a year. We want the grant to encourage Masters and PhD students to undertake research into road safety issues. They could be many and varied, including the effectiveness of road safety advertising and promotion, road safety education, police interventions, teenage drinking and driving, roading design and the psychological and physical influences on driver behaviour.

We hope the grant will yield better quality research into road safety, and ultimately prevent needless deaths on the road. If we can stop one other family from going through what we've been through then it will have done its job.

* * *

What's next? Well, the job has changed a lot since I began in transport. In those days I would drive trucks occasionally to help and shift the bulldozers around the various sites at weekends. I probably worked like that – working mainly from the office but driving a truck when it suited – until the mid-80s. But as we expanded I recognised the need to have good managers in place. They would report to me but it was their job to find the work to keep the company going.

As we grew larger we had regional managers for the concrete operations and they're now spread throughout the country. They all report to Peter Carnahan, a friend of Harold's who used to work part-time for us while he was a partner in a local accounting firm. He's the son of Russell, of the Southland Carrying Company. I still take a personal interest in the transport companies, along with my son-in-law Scott O'Donnell.

Officially my title is governing director. I try to stay out of the market aspects of what the group does, but I like to know about the big jobs that come along, the jobs you can lose your shirt on if your sums are wrong. Mostly, however, I ask only one question: "Are you sure you've got it right?" And I still like to get involved with some of the mechanical problems that come along.

Our business turns over more than $150 million a year. About 53 percent of that comes from concrete sales, 23 percent from fuel sales and distribution, 12 percent from transport and 12 percent from SouthRoads. We spend about $30 million a year on cement. We are Milburn's biggest customer and I often wonder what my father would make of this, given his involvement with Southland Cement and dislike of Milburn at the time.

Shona and Bill Richardson.

We have about 350 heavy trucks on the road plus a large fleet of ancillary equipment, such as 18 graders, lots of rollers, smaller trucks, pickups, 70-odd four-wheel drive front-end loaders and a few hydraulic excavators.

We pay annual wages of more than $20 million and road user charges of just under $4.5 million. To keep our vehicles on the road we spend just under $1 million

131

Joc, Scott and their children.

a year on tyres and $3 million on fuel. Some people say we don't pay our fair share of road expenses. I think we pay more than our fair share.

As I look over our nationwide activities I think we are in very sound financial shape. The company has a lot of good people. As long as people remember where we have come from, keep their feet on the ground, remember what we are here to do, and keep on doing the job – as I have tried to encourage them – I don't think we can go wrong.

I will remain Southland-based with a good, viable company that has enough momentum and size to ensure we have a bit of muscle among the bigger players so we don't get pushed around. We could have been a lot bigger had we spread our ownership and shifted away, while concentrating more on the larger centres. As it is, two-thirds of our business is now outside Southland. But it's questionable whether we would have ended up more profitable, and it really gets back to what you want to achieve in the long run.

The one disadvantage of being based in Invercargill is that you have to travel, although people know where we are. One advantage is that some people elsewhere tend not to take us seriously because of where we come from, and that can help us in negotiating or advancing our businesses. For some strange reason these people think that because you're not based in Auckland or a large city you somehow must be inferior and that they don't need to take you seriously. It's infuriating but it has its pluses.

Southland's an easy place to do business and there's a more relaxed business atmosphere. Above all, Southland suits the way we are. I can oversee the company's operations throughout the country from my office and I can walk home for lunch or morning tea if I want to.

I'm not pleased to be on the National Business Review "rich" list, a meaningless and not necessarily accurate grouping of the so-called wealthy people of this country. It's a sad reflection of the world and its priorities that people are too often judged not so much on the good they might have done but on the wealth they may have accumulated. And it puzzles me that they know how wealthy I am when I don't know myself. What is my business worth? Who knows until I try to sell it.

I'd rather be known as a good employer, good to our staff. I want H W Richardson Group Ltd and its associated companies known as good companies to work for, businesses which always strive to do well, give good service and are fair to everyone they deal with.

If our people remember these things there's no reason why the company can't carry on for many, many years. I'd hate to think we'd get to the stage where we were gobbled up by multi-nationals. In some industries politics come into it but it should be possible to carry on as an independent.

That's the business. Most important of all to me is our family, older generations and new. In later life I have got to know Dad's brother, Bill, who shifted to England in 1953 and spent his life in the construction industry there. On his visits to New Zealand in recent years I have enjoyed his company and have learned a lot of the family history from him.

After Harold was killed we were very fortunate that our daughter, Jocelyn, and her husband Scott decided to return to Invercargill from Christchurch. They have since had two sons, Harrison and Cameron, who are a source of enormous pleasure for us. My wish as a grandfather is that, with Scott in the business, the two boys will also become interested, but that's in the future.

Having Joc, Scott and the boys so close encourages us to be positive. We are also very fortunate in Julie, our daughter-in-law, who we love very much, and who has handled Harold's death so courageously as she gets on with her life.

*   *   *

Our story began with Samuel, my great grandfather, who came to this country as a young man alone. He arrived with very little but he had faith in himself. The land he adopted was good to him and to the family he loved. Samuel was a man who looked to the future and he began our tradition of looking for and taking opportunities. New Zealand has been good to the successive generations of Richardsons and their families as well. We have much to be grateful for.

But there's always work to be done.

APPENDIX 1

MAJOR R RICHARDSON LTD CONTRACTS

Kew Hospital Laundry Block, Invercargill
156 Government houses, Tay, Islington, Millar and Tweed Streets, Invercargill
Southland Farmers Wool Store, Invercargill
Southland Farmers Grain Store, Invercargill
Wright Stephenson and Co Grain Store, Invercargill
Dalgety Wool Store, Invercargill
Wright Stephenson and Co Wool Store Extension, Invercargill
Catholic Church, Wyndham
St Patrick's Catholic Church, Georgetown
Sacred Heart Catholic Church, Waikiwi
Catholic Convent, Nightcaps
St Mary's Presbytery, Nith Street, Invercargill
Calvary Hospital, Invercargill
St Mary's Hall, Invercargill
St Bertrand's Convent, Georgetown
Scottish Hall, Invercargill
Verdon College, Invercargill
Catholic Presbytery, North Invercargill
Dominican Sisters' Convent, View Street, Invercargill
Chemical Works, Pourakino Valley
Tweedsmuir Intermediate School, Invercargill
Tisbury School
Dacre School
Limehills School
Clifton School
Kapuka School
North School, Invercargill, Extensions
Surrey Park School, Invercargill, Extensions
Rosedale Intermediate School, Invercargill
James Hargest High School, Invercargill
Lithgow Intermediate School, Invercargill
Cargill High School, Invercargill
Kingswell High School, now Mt Anglem College, Invercargill
Invercargill City Council Water Treatment Plant, Branxholme
Invercargill City Council Sewage Treatment Plant, Clifton
Invercargill City Council Water Reservoir, Waikiwi
Wyndham Dairy Factory
Tisbury Dairy Factory
Southland Butchers By-Products Plant, Grasmere
Gore Hospital Extensions (our first job worth more than £100,000)
Alliance Freezing Company single men's quarters, Lorneville
Alliance Freezing Company Large Cool Store, Lorneville
Gore Hospital Boiler House
Mataura Meat Plant Boiler House
Ocean Beach Meat Plant Cool Store
Southland Hospital Board Head Office, Victoria Avenue, Invercargill
Phoenix House (Now NZI House), Invercargill
SIMU offices, Invercargill
Police Station, Invercargill
NZR locomotive sheds, Invercargill
Glengarry Tavern, Invercargill
J Lucas Building, Invercargill
J J Niven Building, Invercargill
Smith and Smith Building, Invercargill
Royds Warehouse
Southland Boys' High School Coldstream Hostel
Milburn Cement Silos, Bond Street
Karitane Hospital, North Road, Invercargill
Press Hall, Southland Times, Invercargill
Ward 12, Kew Hospital, Invercargill
Peacehaven PSSA Home, Invercargill
IHC Home, Waikiwi
Ohai Miners' Hostel
NML Building, Invercargill
Andrews and Beavan Building, Invercargill
Commodore Flats, Invercargill
Government flats (six blocks), five houses, Lithgow, Yarrow and Lyon Streets, Invercargill
Several hundred transportable homes

APPENDIX 2

MAJOR ALLIED AND OTHER SUBSIDIARY CONCRETE COMPANY PROJECTS

cubic metres

Tiwai Point Aluminium Smelter Extensions, 1980 and 1997	40,000
Rayonier Fibre Board Plant, Mataura	10,000
Port Chalmers Wharf	8,500
Tauranga Wharf	20,000
Opuha Dam, South Canterbury	14,500
Otira Gorge Viaduct	10,000
Cromwell Gorge Stabilisation Tunnels	70,000
Palmerston North Windmill Farm	3,500
Mercury Energy Tunnel, Auckland	15,000
Auckland International Airport Runway Extensions	18,000
Shakespeare Bay Wharf, Picton	7,500
Auckland South-eastern Arterial Route Motorway	12,000

Left: The SIMU Building in Don Street.

Below: Richardsons timber market and handyman's centre was a familiar sight off Tay Street, Invercargill, for many years.

Top right: The Police Station, Don Street, Invercargill.

Below right: Phoenix House on the corner of Kelvin and Don Streets is a well-known Invercargill landmark.

APPENDIX 3

PLACES OF OPERATION

APPENDIX 4

DIRECTORY

H W Richardson Group

Head Office:
35 Inglewood Road, Invercargill
P O Box 1104, INVERCARGILL
Ph: (03) 217 0990 Fax: (03) 2171077
Website: www.allied-concrete.co.nz
E-mail: allied@hwr.co.nz

Concrete Operations

Readymix Concrete

NORTH ISLAND

Allied Concrete
Henry Rose Place, **NORTH SHORE**
P O Box 97 542,
SOUTH AUCKLAND MAIL CENTRE
Ph: (09) 415 3470 Fax: (09) 415 3475

Allied Concrete
204 Wiri Station Road, **AUCKLAND**
P O Box 97 542,
SOUTH AUCKLAND MAIL CENTRE
Ph: (09) 279 8184 Fax: (09) 279 8208

Allied Concrete
783 Te Rapa Road, **TE RAPA**
P O Box 10 311, HAMILTON
Ph: (07) 849 3422 Fax: (07) 849 7096

Allied Concrete
Redbridge Road, **TAIRUA**
P O Box 83, TAIRUA
Ph: (07) 864 8038 Fax: 864 8039

Allied Concrete
Mirrielees Road, **TAURANGA**
P O Box 432, TAURANGA
Ph: (07) 578 8060 Fax: (07) 577 1034

Allied Concrete
Gateway Drive West, **WHAKATANE**
PO Box 817, WHAKATANE
Ph: (07) 307 0317 Fax: (07) 307 0349

Allied Concrete
Biak Street, **ROTORUA**
P O Box 384, ROTORUA
Ph: (07) 348 0019 Fax: (07) 346 3809

Head Office staff, 1998.

Allied Concrete
Miro Street, **TAUPO**
P O Box 1492, TAUPO
Ph: (07) 378 4281 Fax: (07) 378 9551

Allied Concrete
11 Railway Road,
WHAKATU, HAWKES BAY
P O Box 36, WHAKATU, HAWKES BAY
Ph: (06) 870 1193 Fax: (06) 870 1194

Allied Concrete
Mould Street, **WAITARA**
P O Box 3318, NEW PLYMOUTH
Ph (06) 754 8484 Fax: (06) 758 3210

Allied Concrete
Hurlstone Drive, **NEW PLYMOUTH**
P O Box 3318, NEW PLYMOUTH
Ph (06) 758 5202 Fax: (06) 758 3210

Allied Concrete
Orlando Street, **STRATFORD**
P O Box 3318, NEW PLYMOUTH
Ph (06) 765 7370 Fax (06) 758 3210

Allied Concrete
Scott Street, **HAWERA**
P O Box 667, HAWERA
Ph (06) 278 8966 Fax (06) 278 8966

Allied Concrete
Saunders Road, **OKATO**
P O Box 3818, NEW PLYMOUTH

Allied Concrete
18 Liffton Street, **WANGANUI**
P O BOX 37, WANGANUI
Ph (06) 345 5467 Fax (06) 345 7420

Allied Concrete
Maxwells Line, **PALMERSTON NORTH**
P O Box 40, PALMERSTON NORTH
Ph (06) 354 0488 Fax (06) 353 6165

Allied Concrete
Main South Road, **OHAU LEVIN**
P O Box 205, LEVIN
Ph (06) 368 9109 Fax (06) 368 9080

Allied Concrete
Birmingham Street, **PARAPARAUMU**
P O Box 205, LEVIN
Ph (04) 296 1327 Fax (04) 296 1326

Allied Concrete
Buchanan Place, **MASTERTON**
P O Box 155, MASTERTON
Ph (06) 378 8018 Fax (06) 378 7537

Allied Concrete
State Highway 53, **FEATHERSTON**
Featherston Martinborough Road, RD1
P O Box 155, MASTERTON

Ready Mixed Concrete
Dry Creek Quarry, Haywoods Hill,
LOWER HUTT
P O Box 30 739, LOWER HUTT
Ph (04) 563 6741 Fax (04) 563 6715

Allied Concrete
28 Landfill Road, **WELLINGTON**
P O Box 7345, WELLINGTON
Ph (04) 383 7794 Fax (04) 383 6167

SOUTH ISLAND

Allied Concrete
78 Pascoe Street, **NELSON**
P O Box 1161, NELSON
Ph (03) 548 6695 Fax (03) 546 4625

TRANSIT MIX CONCRETE
(ALLIED MILBURN LIMITED)

Transit Mix Concrete
Lower Queen Street, **RICHMOND, NELSON**
P O Box 9016, NELSON
Ph (03) 543 93373 Fax (03) 543 9394

Allied Concrete
Blenheim Road, **RENWICK**
P O Box 53, RENWICK
Ph (03) 572 8318 Fax (03) 572 9433

Williams-Allied Concrete
Flower Street Extension, **GREYMOUTH**
P O Box 379, GREYMOUTH
Ph (03) 768 6822 Fax (03) 768 7172

Williams-Allied Concrete
Hau Hau Road, **HOKITIKA**
P O Box 379, GREYMOUTH
Ph (03) 755 8739 Fax (03) 755 6170

Williams-Allied Concrete
OTIRA P O Box 379, GREYMOUTH
Ph (03) 738 2882

Allied Concrete
Cnr Railway and Station Road, **RANGIORA**
P O Box 33 144, CHRISTCHURCH
Ph (03) 313 3518

Allied Concrete
14 McAlpine Street, **CHRISTCHURCH**
PO Box 33 144, CHRISTCHURCH
Ph (03) 348 8329 Fax (03) 348 3190

Ashby Concrete
544 Johns Road, **CHRISTCHURCH**
P O Box 5249, CHRISTCHURCH
Ph (03) 359 7084 Fax (03) 359 7082

Allied Concrete
180 Dobson Street, **ASHBURTON**
PO Box 574, ASHBURTON
Ph (03) 308 2399 Fax (03) 308 2383

Allied Concrete
Hilton Highway, **WASHDYKE**
P O Box 2059, TIMARU
Ph (03) 688 2152 Fax (03) 688 2696

Allied Concrete
MAKIKIHI P O Box 2059, TIMARU
Ph (025) 228 9267

Allied Concrete
Cnr Butts Road and Ravensbourne Road,
DUNEDIN P O Box 144, DUNEDIN
Ph (03) 477 0181 Fax (03) 477 0383

Allied Concrete
Ballantyne Road, **WANAKA**
P O Box 142, WANAKA
Ph (03) 443 8366 Fax (03) 443 8367

Allied Concrete
Boundary Road, **ALEXANDRA**
P O Box 257, ALEXANDRA
Ph (03) 448 7704 Fax (03) 440 2005

Queenstown Concrete
Gorge Road, **QUEENSTOWN**
P O Box 956, QUEENSTOWN
Ph (03) 442 7242 Fax (03) 442 8124

Allied Concrete
Charlton Road, **GORE**
P O Box 316, GORE
Ph (03) 208 5249 Fax (03) 208 5245

Allied Concrete
41 Basstian Street, **INVERCARGILL**
P O Box 1104, INVERCARGILL
Ph (03) 215 9129 Fax (03) 215 9103

Concrete Products

Allied Concrete Products
Tweed Street, **INVERCARGILL**
P O Box 1104, INVERCARGILL
Ph (03) 218 6337 Fax (03) 218 6331

Allied Concrete Products
Charlton Road, **GORE**
P O Box 316, GORE
Ph (03) 208 5249 Fax (03) 208 5245

Concrete Containised Tanks Ltd
14 McAlpine Street, **CHRISTCHURCH**
P O Box 31 201, CHRISTCHURCH
Ph (03) 343 3136 Fax (03) 341 3105

TRANSPORT

Rural Transport

Kapuka Transport Ltd
Kapuka South Road, No 5 RD, **KAPUKA**
Ph (03) 239 5854 Fax (03) 239 5824

Herberts Transport Ltd
110 Seaward Road, **EDENDALE**
Ph (03) 206 6580 Fax (03) 206 6583

Transport Services (Southland) Ltd
10 Moffat Street, **NIGHTCAPS**
Ph (03) 225 7893 Fax (03) 225 7029

Hokonui Haulage Ltd
Aparima Street, **GORE.**
P O Box 834, GORE
Ph (03) 208 9050 Fax (03) 208 9997

Andrews Transport (1993) Ltd
Main South Road, **RIVERSDALE**
P O Box 58, RIVERSDALE
Ph (03) 202 5634 Fax (03) 202 5631

Bulk and Specialist Haulage

Southern Transport Co Ltd
92 Otepuni Avenue, **INVERCARGILL**
P O Box 1104, INVERCARGILL
Ph (03) 216 9059 Fax (03) 216 5530

Purdue Bros Ltd
Nith Street, **INVERCARGILL**
P O Box 257, INVERCARGILL
Ph (03) 218 8237 Fax (03) 218 9303

Freight Haulage Ltd
3 Spey Street, **INVERCARGILL**
P O Box 85, INVERCARGILL
Ph (03) 218 2447 Fax (03) 218 3748
E-mail: freight.haulage@hwr.co.nz

Roading and Construction

SouthRoads Ltd
Hunt Street, **INVERCARGILL**
P O Box 968, INVERCARGILL
Ph (03) 215 9191 Fax (03) 215 6038

Fuel Distribution

Allied Petroleum Ltd
14 McAlpine Street, **CHRISTCHURCH**
P O Box 31 201, CHRISTCHURCH
Ph (03) 348 6086 Fax (03) 341 3105
E-mail: allied.petroleum@hwr.co.nz

Gore Services Ltd
7 Oreti Street, **GORE**
P O Box 124, GORE
Ph (03) 208 9355 Fax (03) 208 9372

Other Operations

FERNHILL
LIMEWORKS LTD

Fernhill Limeworks Ltd
Cooney Road, 2 RD, **WINTON**
Ph (03) 236 0879

Allied Materials
Bond Street, **INVERCARGILL**
P O Box 1104, INVERCARGILL
Ph (03) 218 2049 Fax (03) 216 5530

GREENHILLS QUARRY LTD

Greenhills Quarry Ltd
Greenhills, **INVERCARGILL**
P O Box 1104, INVERCARGILL
Ph (03) 212 7159 Fax (03) 212 7159

APPENDIX 5

20-YEAR STAFF

ALLIED CONCRETE LIMITED

Branch	Name
Auckland	Alan Clark
Blenheim	Len Fleurty
	Jim Walker
Christchurch	Robin Gibson
	Paul Rodrigues
	Doug Strachen
Dunedin	Gill Mackinlay
Gore	Vic Botting
	Wayne Richardson
Invercargill	Colin Murray
SCP	John Nieborg
Timaru	Doug Gordon
	Ken MacDonald
	Peter Rose

ALLIED MILBURN LTD

Levin	Gary Coles
	Des Coomes
Rotorua	Dennis Kiff
Taupo	Willie Houia
Tauranga	Len Humphrey
Wellington	Peter Williamson

ANDREWS TRANSPORT LTD

Tom MacPherson
Murray Maslin
Roger McBain
Ian McIntosh
Eugene O'Sullivan
Bruce Stevenson
Fairley Stevenson
Peter Stevenson
Norman Welsh

ALLIED PETROLEUM LTD

Brian Bennison
David Cable
Graeme Joyce
Kevin Penn

FREIGHT HAULAGE LTD

Bernie Bower
Athol Cooper
John King
Trevor Milne
John Searle

GORE SERVICES LTD

Eddie Duncan
Don Graham
Gary Richardson
Marion Neil

GREENHILLS QUARRY LTD

Ross McKinnel
Peter Robjohns

HWR GROUP

Bev Erskine

HERBERTS TRANSPORT LTD

Ken Holland

PURDUE BROS LTD

Ivan Colvin
Chester Martin
John Purdue
Sylvia Purdue
John Roger

SOUTHERN TRANSPORT CO LTD

Mick Cordell
Bill Gilbert
Russell Gorham
Russell Hibbs
Alan McDowall
Ray Phillips
Stuart Robertson
Lewis Templeton

SOUTHROADS LTD

Ivan Butler
Jimmy Clark
Colin Dempster
Ray McIvor
Ed Plaisted
Russell Palmer
Graeme Williams
Charlie Wilson

TRANSPORT SERVICES LTD

John Curtin
Donny McRae
Ian Steel

WILLIAMS – ALLIED CONCRETE LTD

Kevin Carter
Jim McEnaney

APPENDIX 6

CHRONOLOGY OF COMPANY HISTORY

1944	R Richardson Ltd formed
1946	Southern Transport Ltd formed by H G R
1948	R Richardson Ltd bought by H G R
1951	H G Richardson Sons formed to buy farm
1954	Niagara Sawmilling bought by H G R
1960	South Invercargill Transport purchased
1963	Kennington Transport bought
1964	L B McLeod purchased
1965	R Hazlett & Sons purchased
1968	W P Hogan purchased
1971	R J McDowell purchased
	Rimu Transport purchased
1976	J H Thomas & Co (sawmillers) purchased
	Allied Concrete purchased
1977	B H Benneworth purchased
1978	Timaru Readymix formed to buy Winstones plant
1979	Otepuni Transport bulk division bought
1980	G E Tregenza Ltd bought into
	Purdue Bros purchased 66.6% (now wholly owned)
	McNeill Drilling purchased 66.6%
1982	1st split: KGR took R Richardson Ltd and Niagara
	HWR took Southern Transport and Allied Concrete
	Francis Construction Services bins bought by Tregenzas
1983	Freightways Timaru bought in February, sold in March by Tregenzas, keeping only bin side of business
	Bought 50% of Daveys Concrete
1984	Final split: KGR took all farms and McNeill Drilling
	HWR took 66.6% of Tregenzas
	50% Farrier Waimak (now wholly owned)
	66.6% Purdue Bros (now wholly owned)
	66.6% Timaru Readymix Concrete (now wholly owned)
1986	Capital Concrete Ltd formed and Wellington plant built.
	Bought interest in Lloyds Concrete, Alexandra (now wholly owned)
1987	Bought Ashburton Concrete
1988	Sold share of Daveys Concrete
	Bought share in Queenstown Concrete
	Formed Allied Milburn, 50/50 with Milburn NZ and sold Wellington plant to new company (see separate sheet.)
1989	Southland Carrying Co purchased
	Bought share in Marlborough Readymix (Blenheim) (now wholly owned)
	Bought share in Freight Haulage Ltd Invercargill (now wholly owned)
	Bought Rangiora Readymix
1990	Bought Shiel Concrete, Dunedin
	Bought share in Certified Concrete (Nelson) (now wholly owned)
1993	Village Readymix Picton purchased
	Empire Forwarding Co Invercargill purchased
	Bluff Carrying Co purchased
	Bought share in Andrews Transport, Riversdale
	Bought share in Herberts Transport, Edendale
	Bought share in Greenhills Quarry Ltd
1994	Bought A1 City Carriers, Invercargill
	Bought share in King Concrete Ltd, Auckland
1996	Bought rest of King Concrete Ltd, Auckland
	Bought Kapuka Transport
	Transport Services Ltd, Nightcaps purchased
	Wanaka Readymix purchased
	SouthRoads Ltd, Invercargill purchased
	Sold GE Tregenza Ltd
1997	Bought Waikawa-Invercargill Freight Service
	Formed Williams-Allied Concrete Ltd, Greymouth, 50/50
	Commissioned Albany Plant, North Shore, Auckland.
1998	Bought Makikihi Readymix

ALLIED MILBURN LTD FORMED 1988
	Bought Capital Concrete, Wellington, Powell Bros, Tawa and 3 plants ex Firth – Rotorua, Taupo and Tauranga
1990	Bought Speirs Concrete at Levin and Paraparaumu
	Bought Gold Coast Concrete at Otaki
1991	Purchased Waikato Readymix, Hamilton
	Bought Redi-Crete, Palmerston North
1992	Bought Foxton Concrete
	Bought Ashby Bros, Christchurch
1994	Bought Wainui Concrete, Wainuiomata
	Bought Gorrie Bros Concrete, Upper Hutt
	Started in Masterton
1995	Bought Brunton Concrete, Upper Hutt
1996	Bought Tairua Readymix
1997	Bought Ready Mixed Concrete Ltd's plants at Taranaki, New Plymouth, Stratford, Hawera, Waitara
	Started in Whakatane
1998	Started in Whakatu
	Bought Transit Mixed Concrete Ltd, Nelson
1999	Started at Okato, Taranaki
	Started at Featherston (plant nearly complete 9.8.99)

APPENDIX 7

VEHICLES IN TRUCK MUSEUM

August 1999

FORD

1916	Ford T Truck-maker conversion
1924	TT
1930	AA
1932	BB4
1933	BB V8
1937	79
1940	01TF
1946	21TF
1946	69W
1948	F155
1949	F155
1949	F6 COE
1951	F6 Thornton
1955	F100
1949	Fordson 7V
1954	Thames ET6
1954	Thames E83W
1957	Thames 500E
1957	Thames Trader 55
1962	Thames Trader 15
1967	Ford K600

INTERNATIONAL

1926	43
1927	SL36
1930	A4
1933	D1
1936	C30
1936	C40F
1938	D30
1938	DS216T
1947	KS5
1947	KBS6
1948	KBS5
1952	AL160
1955	AR162
1955	RF174
1957	AS110
1957	ASC162
1957	SF174
1958	AS148
1958	AS162
1960	AA164
1961	AACO182
1966	F1800
1974	F5070 SF

CHRYSLER/ROOTES GROUP & PREDECESSORS

1928	Graham Bros OE
1935	Dodge K34V
1936	Dodge LF36
1940	Dodge RX70 Airflow Tanker
1942	Dodge WF32
1960	Dodge F264 (UK)
1938	Fargo FG 4-59
1942	Fargo FK 4-60
1954	Fargo F125A (UK)
1954	DeSoto S64
1934	Commer Centaur
1948	Commer Q465
1949	Commer S222
1949	Commer R741
1955	Commer B357
1963	Commer CADY715 TS3

GERMAN & JAPANESE

1957	Mercedes Benz L312
1967	Nissan 6TW12
1968	Hino ZM

GENERAL MOTORS

1936	Bedford WHG
1937	Bedford WTL
1939	Bedford WLG
1939	Bedford MLZ
1949	Bedford OLB
1950	Bedford MLC
1953	Bedford OLB
1954	Bedford A5LC
1955	Bedford SLCG
1958	Bedford D5LC3
1960	Bedford J3LC2
1961	Bedford J6LC3
1964	Bedford KGLC3
1928	Chevrolet XHLO
1936	Chevrolet XHRD
1937	Chevrolet XHSB
1939	Chevrolet XHJE
1941	Chevrolet XHYR
1947	Chevrolet 6-1543
1948	Chevrolet 7-1543 (2)
1936	Maple Leaf
1936	Oldsmobile OSD
1930	GMC T19B
1941	GMC CCKW 352
1954	GMC W624

LEYLAND AND PREDECESSORS OF BRITISH LEYLAND

1952	Leyland Comet 90 ECO2 1R
1955	Leyland Hippo
1959	Leyland Steer 16 53E
1967	Leyland Beaver 14 BT
1971	Leyland Crusader F41
1948	Austin K4 Series 1
1954	Austin K2 Series 2
1957	Austin 503 FC
1968	Austin FG K60
1934	Morris Commercial CS 13/40
1936	Morris Commercial CS2 13/80
1949	Morris Commercial ECV 13/5
1950	Morris Commercial NCV 13/5
1953	Morris Commercial NVS 13/5
1958	Morris 701
1965	Morris FFK100
1955	Albion Claymore FT27 AEN
1956	Scammell Scarab 6 ton
1966	Scammell Handyman III
1948	Thornycroft Sturdy ZETR6

MISCELLANEOUS AMERICAN

1945	Brockway 78
1937	Diamond T 221D
1939	Diamond T 404 (2)
1939	Diamond T 305S
1939	Diamond T 201
1954	Diamond T 522 HH
1936	Federal 15D
1954	Federal 2902 (2)
1927	Gotfredson 20B
1965	Kenworth L923
1941	Mack DE
1942	Mack EH
1955	Mack B653
1974	Mack R685 RS
1928	REO GA
1929	REO FA
1938	REO 1C4
1941	REO 19B
1930	Relay S11B
1930	Republic F2R
1928	Rugby 401
1931	Studebaker S20
1941	Studebaker M15
1942	Studebaker M15
1938	Stewart 61AE
1966	White 2064
1928	Willys Knight 21

MISCELLANEOUS BRITISH

1931	Singer Industrial 25cwt
1937	Dennis 40/45cwt
1948	Dennis Pax
1953	Trojan 15
1955	Seddon 25cwt
1966	Atkinson T30467C

INDEX AND SOURCES

A

A1 and City Carriers 103
Aitken, Harry 24
Aitken, Harry 30
Albany 89
Alexandra 85
Alice Street, Invercargill 17
Alliance Group 88
Allied Concrete 7, 47, 54-57, 75, 78, 79, 83, 85, 88-90
Allied FH Ltd 85
Allied Milburn 83, 84, 86, 87, 89, 90
Allied Petroleum 99, 100, 103
Allied Views 117
Allis Chalmers bulldozer 31, 122, 123
American Truck Historical Society 129
Andrews and Beavan 31, 123
Andrews, Fred 100
Andrews Transport 100, 101
Anglem Street, Invercargill 26, 28, 31
Annan Street wool store 18
Antico, Tristan 77
ANZ Bank 53
APEC Conference 1999 89
Argyle Station 100
Ashburton 64, 85
Ashburton Concrete 85, 88
Ashby Concrete, Christchurch 84
Ashers Siding 103
Atlantic Oil Company 13
Auckland 89
Auckland International Airport 89
Austin trucks 43
Awarua Bay 46, 48, 49

B

Balclutha 85
Balfour 58
Ballymena 12
Banffshire 11
Bank of New South Wales (later Westpac) 92, 93
Bashford, Joe 109
Bedford trucks 38, 39, 41, 43, 44, 121
Belfast 72
Bennell, Keith 92, 93
Benneworth, Bruce 24
Bettle, Rick 88
Bishop, Alf 100
Bitumix 84, 106, 107
Blackhorn Mill 21, 27, 30, 41, 121, 122
Blackler, Lindsay 115
Blick, Fred 79
Blue Circle Group 82
Bluff 25, 46, 53, 66, 99
Bluff Carrying Company 103
Bob Carriers 103
Botriphne 11
Botting, Vic 109
Boyce, Letitia Linda (Robert's wife) 14
BP Oil 38, 84
Branxholme water treatment plant 20
Brierley Investments Ltd 82
Briscoes 25
Briscoes Hardware Merchants 30, 33
British Pavements Ltd (later Pavroc Holdings) 61-65, 67
Broad, Cliff 56
Bruntons Concrete, Upper Hutt
Buckingham, Tom 41
Burnetts 85
Burnham Military Camp 124
Burrell steam engine 121

C

Cable Price 43
Caltex Oil 33, 38, 98, 100, 125
Calvary Hospital 20
Cambridge 14
Cameron, Keith 53
Capital Concrete Ltd 79-81, 83, 84, 89
Cargill High School 20
Carnahan, Maurice 101
Carnahan, Peter 131
Carnahan, Russell 101, 102, 131
Carpenter, Avon 71, 72
Carpenter, Ron 51, 52, 59
Castrol oil 98
Caterpillar 6D6 51, 122
Central Concrete 84, 89
Certified Concrete Ltd 56, 58, 60, 76-78, 80, 83
Certified Concrete (Nelson) Ltd 85, 88
Challis, Edward 11
Checketts Engineering 26
Chevrolet truck 67
Chisholm Bros, Tokanui 101
Christchurch 62, 64, 67-69, 72, 99,100
Civic Theatre 27
Clark log skidders 125
Clark, Stewart 46
Cletrac bulldozer 31, 41, 121, 123
Clifton Lime Company 33, 34
Clifton Sewage Treatment Plant 20
Clifton School 20
Cloughley, Stan 39
Clouston, John 44
Clyde Dam 85, 86
Coffey, Martin 68-70
Coles hydraulic crane 46, 93
Collett, Jim 38
Colonial Sugar Refineries 77
Comalco Ltd 46
Commer trucks 31, 38-40, 63, 64, 104, 123, 126
Commerce Commission 81, 82
Commercial Bank of Australia 92, 93
Concrete Blocks Southland Ltd (later Vibrapac South Island Ltd) 55
Cordell, Mick 109
Cormack, Sandy 76
Coromandel 120
County Antrim 9, 14
Coutts Island 72
Craigevar farm 75
Craigpine Timber Ltd 118
Crawford, Frank 109
Croswell, Les 50
Crimea Street, Wyndham 10
Crimean War 10
Crinan Street, Invercargill 20
Cruickshank, Sarah Anderson (married Samuel Richardson)11
Cruickshank, William (brother of Sarah) 13
Cummins motors 51
Cunningham Transport 102

D

Dacre School 20
Dahlhoff and King 51
Daimler Chrysler 125
Dairy industry 103
Davey's Concrete, Balclutha 73, 85
David Brown tractors, crawlers 29, 123
De Soto 15
John Deere tractors 123
Department of Housing Construction 17
The Depression 15-17
Detroit Diesel 51
Diamond T truck 15, 35, 124, 128
Disston chainsaws 123
Dodge Perkins trucks 59, 124, 126
Don Street, Invercargill 20
Downer Mining 89
Drake, Murray 45
Drott front-end loader 67
Drummall 9
Drysdale Road, Myross Bush 40
Dummies Beach 49
Dundas, Jack 56
Dunedin 60, 85
Duraphos New Zealand Ltd 87, 88
Dynes, Jim 103

E

Eastern Transport 103
Eaton Fuller 51
Edendale 10, 11, 13, 15, 55, 103
Edgar, Ralph 58
Edgeware Village 70
Elliott, R A 10, 11
Emerson, Charlie 36
Employment Contracts Act 110
Empire Forwarding Company 102, 103
England 25
Europa Oil 98, 99

F

Farmers' Concrete Products 55
Farrelly, Jim 21, 23, 24, 30, 92, 112, 123
Farrier Waimak 68-72, 74
Farrier Waimak 1984 Ltd 72, 74, 85, 88
Fea, Bill 55, 56
Fea Concrete Industries Ltd 55, 56
Fea, Dal 55
Fiat tractors 123
Firth Concrete 78, 80, 83, 84, 86, 87, 89, 119, 120
Fletcher Construction (later Fletcher Challenge) 20, 33, 56, 58, 76-78, 81-85, 87, 88, 118-120
Fletcher, Hugh 88
Fletcher, Sir James 76
Foden trucks 126
Ford trucks
  General 43, 104, 121, 126
  Louisville (later Sterling) trucks 124-126
  Thornton trucks 27, 31, 121, 123
Fordson loader 64
NZ Forest Service 50, 51, 125
Fortification 21, 23, 24
Fortification Timber Company 21, 23, 24
Fortrose 13, 50
Fowler, Les 120
Fowler Traction Engine 121
Foxton 84
Foxton Concrete 84, 89
Francis Construction Services 72, 73
Freightliner trucks 126
Freightways 72, 73
Freightways Timaru 72, 73
Frew, Ian 73
Fulton Hogan Holdings Ltd 62, 68, 72, 73, 83, 85, 103, 106
Fulton, John 68, 71
Fuso trucks 63, 64

G

Garrett stationary steam engine 121
Gedye, Noel 60, 61
Georgeson Bros, Invercargill 33, 67
Georgetown 18
Gillies, John 112
Gillies Ltd, Oamaru 123
Glengarry Tavern, Invercargill 20, 34
GMC trucks 27, 56, 122, 123
Gold Coast Concrete, Otaki 84, 89
Golden Bay Cement Company 71, 76, 81-83, 87
Gordon, Bob 44
Gore 10, 98, 99
Gore Hospital 18
Gore Services Ltd 98-100, 102, 103
Gorge Road Transport 103
Gormack Wilkes Davidson 43, 44
Gorrie Concrete, Upper Hutt 85
Gorrie Concrete, Wellington 80
Grand Hotel, Invercargill 59
Greenhills Quarry Ltd 103
Grosvenor Hotel, Timaru 65
Guildford, Jim 35, 36
Guise, Ian 40, 102

H

Haast Pass 128
Hamilton (city) 84
C W F Hamilton Ltd 46
Hamilton cranes 46
Hanomag crawler 31, 1221
Harold Richardson Memorial Road Safety Students Research Grant 130, 131
Harvey, Brett 104

Hawera 120
Hayes, Joe 18
Haywood, Reg 101, 102
R Hazlett and Sons 40
Heenan, Archie 53
Herbert Street, Invercargill 7
Herberts Transport Ltd 103
Hino trucks 126
A G Hoffman Ltd 46
Hoffman, Gordon, 46, 93, 94
Hogan, Jack 40, 41, 104
Hokonui Haulage Ltd 103
Hokonui Hills 50, 51
Holderbank Group 83
Hollands and Pearman Transport 103
Holms, Henderson 29, 73
Horne, Richard 11
Horowhenua 84
Housing 17, 18
Hunter, Jim 119, 120

I

Inglewood Road, Invercargill 7, 26, 65
Inland Revenue Department 25
International Harvester Company 44, 124-126, 128
International
  18cwt truck15
  1936 C40 F truck 24, 129
  1938 DS216T truck 24, 128
  AA 164 trucks 39
  AACO182 trucks 39
  General 23, 27, 40, 43, 46, 51, 73, 123
  K and KB trucks 104
  Loadstar F1800 truck 39
  Model D1 127, 128
  TD15 bulldozers 49, 51, 123
  Tractors 123
Invercargill 10, 16, 20
Invercargill abattoir 53
Invercargill Airport terminal 20
Invercargill City Council 28, 36, 43, 46, 47, 54
Invercargill Licensing Trust 34
Invercargill tramlines 36
Ireland 9, 10, 25
Isla Bank 53
Islington Street, Invercargill 17
IVECO trucks 126

J

Jack, Charlie 43, 117
James Hargest High School 20
Johnston, Geoffrey 125
Johnston steam engines 121
Jones, Stan 103

K

Kapiti Coast 84
Kapuka School 115, 116
Kapuka Transport 103, 104
Karitane Hospital, Invercargill 20
Karrier trucks 38
A J Kelly Ltd 56
Kelman, Bryan 77
Kennedy, Les 109
Kennington sawmill 41, 42, 43, 50
Kennington Transport 39, 40, 41
Kenworth trucks 51, 126
Kerr, Jim 38
Kettle, Cyril 79, 116
Kew (Southland) Hospital 16, 17
Kidd, Snowy 35, 36

Kilkelly Timber Mill 50
King Concrete 89
King, Dave, of D T King, 39, 98, 104
King, Frank 10
King, Tom 40, 43
Kingsland Biscuit Factory, Invercargill 20
Kingswell High School 20
Korean War 29

L

Labour Government 17, 18
Laing, Lynton 54, 57
Land Transport Safety Authority 130
Landfill Road, Wellington 78, 80
Leahy's Hotel, Wyndham 12
Levin 84
Leyland trucks 43, 126
  Crusader 45, 51
  Super Comet 39, 104
Lindsay and Dixon 122
Linklater, Jack 93
Lithgow Intermediate School 20
Lloyds Concrete, Alexandra 85, 88
David Lloyd and Co 41, 130
Lloyd, John 103, 104
Lloyd, Les 103, 115
London 10
Lorneville saleyards 53

M

Macaulay, Bob 32
Macaulay Motors, Invercargill 32
McCall, Robin 103
McDonald, Graham 102-104
McDonald, Samuel 102
S McDonald and Co 102
McDowall, Bob 40, 43, 104, 115
McGregor, Noel 32
McGoldrick Jim 36, 101
MacIvor, Mac 33
MacKay, Peter 103
McKenzie, Graham 50, 51
McKenzies' Department Store 20
McKerchar, Shona (wife of Bill Richardson—see Shona Richardson) 40
McLean, Tom 98, 99
McNeill Drilling 73, 74, 79
McRae, Jack 104
S and J McRae Ltd 104
Mack trucks
  First purchases 51, 52
  General 59, 73, 124-126
Mactrol oil 98
Makikihi 120
Makikihi Transport 120
MAN trucks 126
Manapouri Power Scheme 46
Manpower regulations 19
Manukau 89
Marlborough 85
Marlborough Readymix 85, 89
Marshall portable steam engines 121
Martin, Tommy 67
Maslin, Murray 100, 101
Masterton 85
Mataura 46, 50, 100
Mataura Ensign 12, 13
Mataura Island 13
Mataura River 9, 10
Matchbox toys 59
F and S Maxted Ltd 103
Maxted, Frank 103
Maxted, Sid 103
Meat industry 10, 29, 53
H E Melhop Ltd 31, 121
Mercedes trucks 43, 45, 51, 123, 126

Mercury Energy 89
Milburn Cement 33, 34, 76, 78, 83, 89, 90, 120, 131
Millar Street, Invercargill 17
Mimihau Stream 9
Ministry of Transport 27
Ministry of Works 17
MM Transport 103
Mobil 98-100, 103
Mokoreta 15, 30, 41, 121, 122
Mokoreta-Tahakopa Road, 41
Morris Commercial truck 67, 101
Motor Truck Distributors 51, 59
Mount Linton Station, Western Southland 32
Mount Maunganui 71
Muggeridge, Ian 125
Muir, Miss 112
Mull of Kintyre 9
Munro, Burt 23
Murdoch, Bert 23, 24
Murdoch, Walter ("Chou") 114, 115
Murray, Colin 109

N

National Business Review 133
NCK Crane 46, 93
Neiborg, John 116
Nelson 85
Ness Street, Invercargill 17, 20
New Plymouth 120
New Zealand 9, 10
Niagara Sawmilling Company 21, 23, 24, 27, 30, 31, 38, 73, 74, 92, 112, 121, 122
Nightcaps 18, 104
Nightingale Street, Wyndham 10
Nissan trucks 126
Normanby beach, Timaru 64
North, Alan 39
North Channel 9
North School extensions 20
North Shore 89
Northern Ireland 9, 10, 14
Northern Southland Transport Holdings Ltd 85
Lord Nuffield (Nuffield Corporation)112

O

O'Donnell, Scott 131-133
O'Hara's Concrete, Wanganui 120
Oamaru 55
Ohai Miners' Hostel 18
Oporo 47, 54
Oreti River 46, 47, 54, 59
Otago 11
Otaio 120
Otaki 84
Otara 15
Otautau 55
Otepuni Transport 66
Ower, Nigel 125
Owhiro Bay 78, 83

P

Palmer, Jim 118-120
Palmers Readymix, Dunedin 60, 85, 118-120
Palmerston North 84
Paraparaumu 84
Paterson, Clem 62-65, 68
Paterson, Graham 68
Pavroc Holdings 65, 68, 69-72
Peacehaven Old People's Home 20
Pearce, Alf 24

Pearson, Hamish 73
Pebbly Hills 50
Perriam and Moyles Ltd 104
Phillips, Ray 109, 110
Phoenix House, Don/Kelvin Streets (now NZI House), Invercargill 20
Pioneer Concrete Ltd 77
Placemakers 83
Police Station, Invercargill 20
Pope Bros 102
Port Chalmers container wharf 11, 119
Porter, Frank 93
Pound Road, Yaldhust, Christchurch 72
Powell Bros, Tawa 80, 81, 83, 84
Precision Concrete, Timaru 62, 64
Progress Valley 49-51, 64, 73
Progress Valley Mill 21, 23, 24, 27, 30, 41, 43, 44, 121, 122
Purdue Bros 66-68, 74, 101, 103
Purdue, George 66, 67
Purdue, John 67, 68
Purdue, Syd 66, 67

Q

Queenstown Concrete 85

R

Railways (New Zealand) 20, 27, 41, 62
Raines, Lloyd 34
Rangiora Readymix 89, 120
Ravensdown Fertiliser 87
Readymix concrete
  History 55, 56, 76, 77
Readymix Concrete Ltd 77, 120
Redan 10, 15
Redi-crete 84
Reliable Finance 98
REO truck 23, 104
Renault trucks 126
H W Richardson Group Ltd 7, 74, 100, 131-133
R Richardson Ltd 19, 20, 25-32, 35-37, 39, 64, 65, 71, 73, 74, 91, 92, 121, 122
Richardson, Archibald (son of Samuel) 13
Richardson, Charles (son of Robert) 12
Richardson, Douglas (son of Robert) 14, 16
Richardson, Gary 99
Richardson, George 13
Richardson, Harold George (father of Bill, son of Robert) 7, 13, 15-19, 21, 23-26, 28, 29-41, 45, 65, 91-93, 116, 123, 128
Richardson, Harold William (Bill)
  Allied Concrete takeover 54-60
  Banks and financial institutions 90-97
  Born 20
  Company split 73, 74
  Education 36
  Expansion in readymix concrete 78-89
  Eventual interests 131, 132
  Growing up 7, 8, 21, 29, 35, 36
  Married 40
  Southern Transport early involvement 38-45
  Starting work 31, 36, 37
  Tiwai Point roading contract 46-49

147

Richardson, Harold (son of Bill and Shona) 41, 59, 64, 79-81, 83, 105-109, 118, 119, 125, 127-131
Richardson, James (brother of Samuel) 12
Richardson, Jane (daughter of Samuel, later Mrs Osborne Mackay) 13
Richardson, Jocelyn (daughter of Bill and Shona) 41, 132, 133
Richardson, John (brother of Samuel) 12
Richardson, Joyce (nee Wensley, wife of Harold, mother of Bill) 20, 29, 35, 37, 65, 108
Richardson, Julie (wife of Harold, son of Bill and Shona) 107, 108
Richardson, Ken (brother of Bill, son of Harold) 20, 21, 29, 35-38, 45, 57-60, 65, 73, 74, 92-95, 128
Richardson, Letitia Linda (nee Boyce, wife of Robert, grandmother of Bill) 14, 15, 30
Richardson, Robert (son of Samuel, father of Harold, grandfather of Bill) 11, 13-19, 21, 24, 25, 30, 31, 128
Richardson, Robert (brother of Samuel) 12
Richardson, Ross (son of Ken, nephew of Bill) 120
Richardson, Samuel 9-13, 133
Richardson, Samuel, (brother of Harold, uncle of Bill) 36
Richardson, Sarah Anderson (nee Cruickshank) 10-13
Richardson, Shona (nee McKerchar, wife of Bill) 40, 41, 65, 78, 127, 130, 131, 133
Richardson, William (brother of Samuel) 12,13
Richardson, William (son of Samuel) 13
Richardson, William (son of Robert) 15-17, 19
Richwhite, C M 130
Rimu Transport 40, 43, 51, 104, 117
River Shingle and Sand 1935 Ltd 77
Riversdale 100, 101
Road Transport Alliance/ Association 53, 104, 105
Roberts Concrete 71
Roberts, Ted 36
Roberts, Tom 36
Robertson, Stu 109
Rocklands Farm 46, 73, 93, 115
Rooney, Gary 106
Rosedale Intermediate School 20
Ross, Alister 47
Ross Transport 103
Roxburgh Hydro-Electric Scheme 33, 34
Russell, Vernon 31
Russley Hotel, Christchurch 72

S

Sacred Heart Catholic Church, 18
St Mary's Hall, Invercargill 18
St Patrick's Church, Georgetown, Invercargill 18, 19
Saurer engines 67
Scania trucks 126
Scherp, Ron 39, 43
Scotland 9, 11
Shakespeare Restaurant, Christchurch 78
Shaw, Samuel 14, 15
Shiel Concrete, Dunedin 85, 88, 119, 120
Shilling Carriers 101, 102
SIMU building, Invercargill 20
Singer Carriers 101, 102
Skinner, Keith 55, 57
Smith, Albert 118-120
Smith, John 118-120
Sockburn 72
Sodestrom, "Scandy" 24
Soper, Dougal 59
South Invercargill Transport Company 38
South Otago 10
Southern Transport 7, 24, 27, 32, 35, 38-45, 66, 74, 98, 103, 121, 128, 129
SouthFert (formerly Southland Co-operative Phosphate Co Ltd) 66, 103, 118
Southland Boys High School 7, 36
Southland Carrying Company 36, 101, 131
Southland Cement Company 33, 34, 55, 131
Southland Concrete Products Ltd 55, 79, 116
Southland County (later District) Council 28, 41, 106, 107
Southland Drivers Union 59,110
Southland Freight Haulage Ltd 102, 103
Southland Frozen Meat Ltd 54, 101, 102
Southland Girls High School 27, 40
Southland Sand and Gravel Ltd 33, 56
Southland Times, The 103
SouthRoads 106, 107
Speirs Concrete, Levin 84, 89
Standard Timber Company 21
State Housing, 17-21, 37
Steel Road, Lorneville 40
Stevenson, Peter 100, 101
Stevensons, Auckland 41
Stewart, Dick 53
Stewarts Transport 100
Storer, Alan 128-129
Story, Colin 16
Stratford 120
Stresscrete 83, 118
Studebaker truck 23
Sunbeam Alpine car 53
Surrey Park School 20, 36
Swaney, Jim 52, 53
Swinton Street, Invercargill 24

T

Tairua, Coromandel 120
Taranaki 120
Tattersfield, Trevor 106
Tauranga 71
Tawa 80
Tay Street, Invercargill 17
T R Taylor Ltd 23
Te Peka Farm 29, 31
Te Peka Timber Company 21, 23
Templeton, Lew 109
Thames Trader trucks 31, 32, 39, 40, 58, 123
Thomas and Co 50, 51
Thorneycroft trucks 36, 101
Timaru 15, 60, 62, 63, 72, 73
Timaru Readymix 62, 74, 76, 85, 88
Timberjack log skidders 125
Tisbury Dairy Factory 20
Tisbury School 20, 26
Titan Bluestreak chainsaws 123
Tiwai Point Aluminium Smelter 46, 59, 102, 103
Tokanui 23, 27, 41, 103
Toma, Joe 109, 113, 114
Transit Mixed Concrete 56
Transpac 102, 104
Treaty of Waitangi 9
Tree Farmer log skidders 125
E G Tregenza Ltd, Timaru 60-65, 68, 72-74, 87, 105, 106
Tregenza, G E 63
Truck Museum, Inglewood Rd, Invercargiill 127-129
Tulloch, Ian 103
Tulloch, Mac 46-49, 55, 103
Twain, Mark 117
Tweed Street, Invercargill 17, 19
Tweedsmuir Intermediate School 19, 36

U

Underwood 53
United Concrete 41
United Plant Hire 46, 93
Universal Farm Machines 43, 44
University of Otago 130
Upper Hutt 85

V

Valli, Bill 67
Venlaw Station 16
Verdon College 20
Vibrapac South Island Ltd 55, 56, 60, 62
Vincent, Neville 56-59
Volvo trucks 126
VTR Motors 31

W

Waikaia 100, 101
Waikato Readymix 84, 89
Waikiwi 18
Waikawa Valley 21
Waikawa Freight 24, 104
Waikawa Valley Road 41
Waimahaka 13, 23, 50
Wainui Readymix 84
Wainuiomata 84
Waiouru 108
Waitaki hydro-electric scheme 17
Waitara 120
Walker, Fred 39
Wallis, George 128
Wanganui 120
Washdyke (near Timaru) 60, 87, 88
Watts and Grieve 101, 112
Webb Stark and Co 112
Wellington 78
Wellington City Council 78
Wellington (vessel) 11
Wellington Street, Invercargill 26
Wensley, Joyce (married Harold Richardson - see Richardson) 20, 108
Wensley, Julie (married Harold, son of Bill and Shona-see Richardson) 107, 108
WestpacTrust Bank 92, 93, 96-97
White, Bill 43
White trucks 121
Wilkins and Davies Ltd 46, 48, 49
Wills, Ted 79
Wilson Bros, Invercargill 121
General Windham 10
Winstones Ltd 56, 60-63, 76-78, 80-83, 85, 89, 119
Winton 55
Winton Presbyterian Church 40
Withington and McGoldrick 101
Woodlands 51
World War 1 13, 15
World War 2 19, 124
Wright Stephenson and Co (later Wrightsons) 15, 87, 88
Wyndham 9, 10, 11, 12, 13, 14, 15, 16, 17, 41
  Catholic Church 15
  Dairy factory 15
  Valley 13
Wyndham Farmer (newspaper) 11, 12

Y

Yaldhurst 71
Young, Venn 50

PHOTOGRAPHIC SOURCES
Barry Harcourt
Delmar Studios
Arthur Bremford
Hazledines Studios
Otago Daily Times

WRITTEN SOURCES
Southland Times
Otago Daily Times
Wyndham Farmer
Mataura Ensign
NZ Official Year Book
H W Richardson Group company records
Encyclopaedia Britannica
The History of the McKay Family of Wyndham by M. Noeline Shaw

Special thanks to Miss Madge McKay for archived family material.

Text: 10.5/12 Palatino
Layout by Craig Printing Company Limited from typesetting supplied
Paper: 130gsm Matt Art
Book jacket: 170gsm Art, laminated
Book layout and jacket design: Ellen van Empel
Printed by Craig Printing Company Limited, Invercargill, New Zealand.